KELAMENTER M. SMITH

Living

Beyond

Self

Searching For Meaning

Kelamenter M. Smith

LIVING BEYOND SELF:
Seaching For Meaning

Copyright © 2020 by Kelamenter M. Smith

All rights reserved. This book is protected under the copyright laws of the United States of America. This book may not be copied or reprinted for commercial gain or profit. The use of short quotations or occasional page copying for personal or group study is permitted and encouraged.

Published in Fort Washington, Maryland by:

PERFECTO SOLUTIONS PUBLISHING

Perfecto Solutions Publishing is a division of Perfecto Solutions, LLC. Perfecto Solutions, LLC provides a wide-range of services. To find out more, please go to perfecto-solutions. com.

Scriptures taken from the HOLY BIBLE, New International Version®, (NIV), Copyright © 1973, 1978, 1984 by International Bible Society.

Scriptures taken from the New King James Version®, (KJV), Copyright © 1982 by Thomas Nelson. Used by permission. All rights reserved.

Scriptures taken from the Holman Christian Standard Bible,® (HCSB), Copyright © 1999, 2000, 2002, 2003, 2009 by Holman Bible Publishers.

ISBN: 978-0-578-63062-5

Cover design: Enhanced by Perfecto Solutions Publishing

Edited: Heather Romanowski, Book Realm Revisions, LLC

Printed in the United States of America

SPECIAL ACKNOWLEDGMENT

TO MY MOTHER

Thank you for your love, support, and prayers it is greatly appreciated. You have always encouraged us to strive for better, no matter what comes our way.

ACKNOWLEDGMENTS

Heavenly Father, I thank you for being Sovereign. Thank you for selecting me to write and publish these types of books. I recognize books are neither about my circumstances nor me, but for others to see your infinite power. You get all the glory and all the praise. You are an AWESOME GOD, who deserves more than lip service, but a life that reflects Christ.

I would like to express deep gratitude to my love, my best friend, and husband Eric for all your love and faithful support. Thank you for always standing by me and supporting my dreams. I Love You Darling! My prayer is that God continues to pour into you and to keep you always.

To my sons and daughters: DeMark, Damon, Natasha, and Danielle; I thank you for your loving support. I love you and pray that God will stir up the gifts in you. Seek God above all else and the blessings will follow.

God loves you!

To my granddaughters Jayde and Sunny, Nana loves you and can't wait to see what God has in store for your life. My prayer is that you pursue God with all your heart and might. Stand firm in your faith and know that your family is praying with and for you.

To my sisters, thank you for your continuous love, support, and prayers. Remember that God has your best interest at heart, just trust Him. *"Yet in all these things we are more than conquerors through Him who loved us"*, (Romans 8:37).

To my many adopted children, I pray that God will keep you and shake up everything in your life that keeps you from Him. *"Seek the Lord while He may be found; Call upon Him while He is near"* (Isaiah 55:6), there is nothing too hard for God ~ Trust Me.

I would like to express gratitude to all my families and friends (natural and spiritual). Thank you for the love, prayers, and support through it all and some. I value your concerns and encouraging words, it is truly appreciated very much.

To all my mentors that poured into me, I thank you for all the knowledge, wisdom, prayers, and loving support you have given me. You are truly a treasure and loved. Thank you for taking the time to share in this journey. Yet trusting in the process while moving forward, I'm in a "NO HOLDS BARRED" in Christ.

I would like to acknowledge my prayer partners, who stood in the gap for me, for my family, for this project, for those who will read this book, for those who may not read this book and for those who will browse through this book, Thank you!

There are still countless others, I would like to thank for your timeless efforts to inspire, encourage, protect, and how you humored me. I do cherish you in all that you do for the building up of others for Christ. Please continue to follow hard after Christ and know that all of your labor is not in vain.

Love you much!

DEDICATION

*Y*ou carried me outside your womb and helped raise me as your own. I love and appreciate you. You have stood by my side and have been there when things got tough. To my other Mother who has always been there for others, I dedicate this book to you and say "Thank You" for being more than a mother and aunt, but a loving woman who loves God ~ Pinkey L. McCurtis.

To the late Bishop Steven Bennett Sr.

Thank you for the inpouring of love, wisdom, knowledge, and understanding of God's Word. Thank you for the prayers and concerns you had for our growth in God. I am honored to have been a part of your journey.

You are truly missed!

CONTENTS

Introduction	1

MORNING

Intercession	5
Arise, Arise	7
Hello Sunshine	8
Morning Confessions	9
The Break of Dawn	10
My Delight Is In You	11

HEARTS WORSHIP & INSPIRATIONS

The Unfolding Favor	13
Words of Wisdom	14
My God is Able	15
Hope for Tomorrow	17
A Prophet's Cry	18
Beautiful You Are	20
When God Calls You Faithful	21
When God gives You a New Song to Sing	22
My Grace Is Still Sufficient	23
Grace and Mercy Beyond Measure	25
Soak me in Healing Waters	27

CONTENTS

A Prayer from Me to You	28
Love Is	30
Just Because	31
Streams of Blessings	32
My Prayer	34
On Bended Knees	36
Hello Halo	38
Touched by An Angel	39
Free	40
Sweet Melodies	41
Let's Stay Together	42
Seasons Always Change	43
Savoring The Moments	45
Talking to the Father	47
A Reflection of You	49
The Flow	51
Gratitude	52
Restore Me O Lord	54
Anew	55
The Flow	56

CONTENTS

Crossing Jordan	58
Love Without Cost	59
Beautiful Wings	61
If I Close My Eyes	63
In Pursuit of My First Love	65
By The Way.... I Love You	66
Why I Smile	68

STRENGTH LETTERS

Dear Friend	70
RE: Dear Friend	72
Sincerely Yours	74
Yours Truly	75
Just1Call@Heaven.GOD	77
Diary of a Miscarriage	79

PERSEVERANCE

Building A Better You	82
Plagued By Disgrace	83
Beyond Reason: "Pray 'til it Come"	85
Reflective Memories	86
Hello Operator	88

CONTENTS

Moving Forward	90
The Battle	92
Counterfeit	93
Treading the Trenches	94
Work on Me	96
Beloved	98
Around The Town	99
By The Way	101
To Sir, With Love	102
In God We Trust	104
Don't Forget The Bacon	106
Hold Fast to Your Dream	107
Pain Knows No Name	108
Let My Work Speak For Me	109
Helping Others	110
Million Dollar Prize	112
Out The Backdoor	114
I've Fallen and I Can't Get Up	116
When Words Cut Deep	118
In Secret	119
Don't Throw in The Towel	121
Do You See What I See?	122

CONTENTS

The Great Escape	124
And All Things Were Made New	126
Now I Know	127
Don't Run Away From Me	129
T.A.P. (Trust, Apply, Power)	131
When Life's Pressure Points are Pushed	133
Surrender, Retreat, or Stand Strong	135
Now This	137
Failure Is Not an Option	139
Nothing Else Matters	140
Tough as Nails	141
Deeply Wounded, But I'm Not Broken	142
See It Before It Happens	144
Heaven Knows	146
I'm In Too Deep	147
Cry No More	148
Broken Pieces	150
Healed And Redeemed	151
Look Again	152
The Wake-Up Call	153

CONTENTS

Desperately Seeking Jesus	154
Icebreaker	156
This Time I'll Win	158
The Seasons Of Life	159
Get Up and Get Movin'	160
Against All Odds	161
Mission Accomplished	162
Recovery	164
This Fight Is Not Mine	165
Tell The Story	166
The Struggles Within	167
Yet Holding On	168
The Problem With Me (Inside A Troubled Mind)	170
What Matters Most	172
Why	174
What Kind of Legacy Will You Leave?	176
Another Days Journey	178
Ingenious Decisions	180
I Didn't Know	181
I Tried	182
Self-Destruction	184

CONTENTS

Lord, Hold It All Back	185
Reach Out and Touch	187
In The Midnight Hour	189
You Seem Far Away	190
The Willow Tree Tears Touch Me	191
Daily I Walk	192
The Value of Me	194
From The Crib, They Cry	196
The Silent Killer	198
Fill This Empty Vessel	200
The Price Was Paid: Not By You But For You	202
I See Nothing's Changed	204
Step Aside	207
Discolorations	209
My Flesh Went Suicidal	211
All Glamour but No Brains	212
The Wanderer	213

CONTENTS

The Barren Tree	215
The End-Results	217
The Unthinkable	218
This Fight Just Got Real	220
Do You Care?	222
Sweet Dreams	223
When The Tears Seems To Flow	225
Wake Me When This Is Over	226
Flashbacks Are Heavy Hitters	227
Final Farewell To Your Past	228
In Search Of Me	229
Under Pressure	231
Sudden Impact	232
Rescue Mission	234
The Upside Down Of Things	236

INTRODUCTION

THE STORY AS IS: TAKE IT OR LEAVE IT

We see how the times have changed, even the very essence of who we are and where we came from. Too many lives have suffered for being who we are. Does it really matter about the color of our skin?

We often hear that "Whatever **doesn't kill you makes you stronger.**" Yet, it makes one wonder if this is true for all or has it become vague in the minds of those that were already defeated.

As we look at past to present generations, are we really living up to the potential that was laid out before us. Have we laid aside our heritage for the dollar? Did we honestly contribute anything positive in our society that would display a positive change? Can you truly say you see it now?

We hoped for a better future, but what exactly have we done toward that future? Have we wasted away or downgraded our gifts and talents to appcase others inadequacy? Have we considered the road that lies ahead, in fear that those poisonous words that was once spoken is our reality?

Kelamenter M. Smith

Introduction

What have you gained or lost that would cause you to lose your self-worth? Don't you know that you are valuable and your life has meaning, your testimony is someone else's recovery? I mean, who can heal on their own—No One. Everyone need someone for a reason, a positive reason. We can make this about God, about Jesus Christ, or even about religion, but it's about You.

Whether you believe in God or not, it is your choice. Whether you believe in Jesus Christ or not, it is your choice. Whether you believe in the Holy Spirit or not, it is your choice. **But I do.**

What makes a person different is their unique makeup? Everyone was created differently on purpose, for a purpose. It would be boring if we were all-alike. What would be the purpose in that? Yet the world would spend millions of dollars trying to recreate from the original—why? Could it be some deep down feeling of inadequacy that would prompt for this action to be even considered? Or is there a feeling of being demeaned by those of your peers?

The very ones who release the most hatred acts have either been taught to hate or have experience hate whether it is directly or indirectly. It's been passed down from generation to generation and now has twists and turns. The operations of this world are affected by this monstrous behavior; then collaborate it with ill intent, greed, money, and power—it is a mixture for disaster for all.

By now you are wondering what my reasons for writing all this are and for what; find out your reason for being here. What is your purpose in this life that you can contribute to make this world better? Find your true nature for why you were born in this era in time, not for what man wants you to be–but for what you were created to be.

We all have a predestine journey on this earth for a set purpose. My path may not be your path–but it should move in the flow of making the world a better place. My journey is to be a Kingdom Builder and if I have not projected a lifestyle that will lead someone to Christ—I have failed.

In life, we will have our share of favorable and unfavorable seasons. But in those seasons, we should not get lost in them nor lose who we are and our purpose for being on this earth.

Morning

Cause me to hear Your lovingkindness in the morning, for in You do I trust.

Psalm 143:8

Kelamenter M. Smith

INTERCESSION

Abba Father, all glory and honor is yours alone. We bless your holy and righteous name. We magnify you and adore you. You are our El Shaddai, our Jehovah-Elyon, our Strong Tower, our Chief Cornerstone, the Alpha, and the Omega. Hallelujah!

Abba Father, forgive us of every distraction, every weight, and doubt that we allowed to hinder us, those things that kept us from reaching out to you. Father in the name of Jesus, we ask that you create in us a pure heart and place in us a right spirit. We desire to be more like Jesus. Teach us how to walk boldly in Your Word and in this world.

Abba Father, we desire your truth and your truth will set us free. Release in us the fruits of your spirit. Release your Holy Spirit to guide us and nurture us in walking out our purpose. Abba Father, teach us how to number our days to be obedient unto you, show us how you see us, and the plans you have for our life. Teach us how to love ourselves, others, and most of all you, show us the desires of your heart.

Abba Father, you are the Great I AM and there is none like you. No one can do what you did; there is no greater love than the love you have for us. We thank you for showing us what true love looks like. Abba Father, we take delight in you and comfort in your word. We will put our trust in you. Your word says, "You'll never put more on us than we can bear." How much more O God must we endure? Please give us the strength to stand a little while longer.

Abba Father impress upon our hearts and minds, your words of healing, deliverance, favor, and protection while we go through the turbulence of life. Let your peace that surpasses all understanding guard our hearts and minds. Keep us O Lord in your secret place and let us remain in your embrace, it is in Jesus name we pray—Amen.

ARISE, ARISE

Arise, Arise O morning dew.
Arise, Arise, and give God praise.
Arise with the breath of Life and give God the glory
For the Lord God is worthy of all praise and glory.

Arise, Arise early in the morning I will praise you.
Arise, Arise late in the evening I will praise you;
Even in the midday, I will praise you.
Arise, Arise every able body and praise Our Majesty.

Arise, Arise little children and praise the Lord God.
Arise, Arise O Israel and praise the Lord God Almighty.
Arise, Arise all of God's people and give Him the glory.
With every breath you take, give our Creator praise.
For there is none like Him, with our whole heart let's give God praise!

*"Let everything that hath breath praise the Lord.
Praise ye the Lord.*

(Psalms 150:6 KJV)."

Kelamenter M. Smith

Morning

HELLO SUNSHINE

Hello sunshine, hello new day!
>We welcome you on this lovely day!
>
>We bid you to shine your radiant rays our way.
>
>To help make this a brighter day.
>
>Hello sunshine, hello new day!
>
>We welcome you on this blessed day!
>
>To make new beginnings and silence the old.
>
>To make peace and joy our Heavenly abode.
>
>Hello sunshine, hello new day!
>
>No matter what may come our way!
>
>It will still be a sunny day.
>
>Awaiting your smile,
>
>So, will you smile today?
>
>And thank God for another day to fulfill
>His heart's desire!

Kelamenter M. Smith

MORNING CONFESSIONS

Oh Heavenly Father, how I long for days and nights like this with you. You have intrigued me more than any other and I would not have it any other way.

Oh Heavenly Father, how I love these moments with You. It takes my breath away and it soothes my soul. Even when I don't know what to say You already know. I do Love You.

From the depths of my heart, my soul longs for you to be with me always. No matter where I am, I am seeking you always. You are the reason I live.

Oh, Heavenly Father, I thank you for your sweet essence that kisses me in the morning and covers me in the night. You send your angels to watch and fight for me while I am weak. No one can compare to you. You are my One and Only God.

Thank You for loving me!

THE BREAK OF DAWN

It is those quiet mornings that I seek your face. Searching for answers to my personal questions only you can handle. It is those peaceful moments that I bathe in your presence. It is there my days and nights are sweet and filled with unspeakable joy.

Early in the morning is the best time for me and you without the worlds' interruptions made by you-know-who. I am at my best when we meet, but when I don't meet you, I miss you.

It is those pleasurable dreams that oftentimes seem unreal, but it's not impossible to be fulfilled. It is my reason for early morning meditation, to gain instruction, knowledge, and whatever the Father wants to share with me.

It is those special occasions that make me feel the way I do. It is the break of dawn that I'm longing for you, your touch, and your gentle breath. It is there I am blessed and refreshed from stress, living fancy free.

Early in the morning is the best time for me and you. I am grateful for all that you do. My life has no meaning without you, which is why I love meeting up with you? Each time we meet I feel brand new!

MY DELIGHT IS IN YOU

When I wake-up to the morning dew, your smile touches me gently.

The warmth of your embrace envelopes me in your durable arms.

And treat me like a queen and you're my superstar.

In the morning mist, I find you there.

Surrounded by your glorious glow.

Filled with hopes and dreams that are fulfilled one by one each day.

Your presence makes me feel in awe whatever comes my way.

You whisper my name and I stand in salute to you.

Tell me what it is I can do for you that I may bring you joy through the many facets of my living.

May my life bring you pleasure and not shame, just to know

I put a smile on your face and delight myself in you!

Kelamenter M. Smith

Hearts, Worship & Inspirations

A Heart of Worship

I will praise You, O Lord my God, with all my heart.   Psalm 86:12

Kelamenter M. Smith

THE UNFOLDING FAVOR

God, grant me this day where your grace looks straight at me. Grant me this day that I walk daily in peace. Hold me in your protective arms after I fall from your way. Teach me to learn from your unfolding favor and love.

Lord, I tried it my way and nothing went accordingly. I tried to do it without you, but the enemy knew all too well. I'm sorry I didn't listen nor follow your plan. Now I understand that you know what's best for me, You, Oh Lord Almighty control the land.

Thank you for allowing me to learn from my mistakes, and not handing me over to the devil's advocate. From this day forward, I am searching your Word, if nothing is aligned to you, I don't want anything to do with it.

Lord, I'm tired of failing and falling short; life dealt with me hard. I thought I could handle whatever came my way but I was lying to myself. Wounded, bruised, and weary, I became but not broken. So, I come you to be whole, safe, and secure again never leaving you again.

Thank You Lord for your mercy and love that still covers me!

WORDS OF WISDOM

Reflecting on past hurts, pains, and disappointments only hurt and hinder your present. You have to release that past hurt and pain in order for God to move you forward, ask me how I know. God is moving me forward and I feel sensational. Come and join us for an Oh Break Out experience and feel renewed: gaining strength, courage, and a new direction through Christ Jesus.

It is AWESOME!

MY GOD IS ABLE

When the weight of the world seems too hard to bear, when the load of weariness seems to overshadow you; and has you bound while no one seems to care. Take it all to the throne and know that the Savior cares.

When the pressures of life get the best of you and it's hard to stay afloat. When the chains get too strong to break and your tears have been your source. Know that the Master has every concern in control, you don't have to hide. Yes, the Father knows what you're up against, but He also knows what's in you to succeed.

Heaven is waiting on you to breakthrough and become free. There's power in you, although you might deny. You may feel as though you can't make it this round or another night. Don't give up; you can make it, just trust in Him, the True Almighty King seated in Glory. You have been called from darkness into the light, now it's up to you to stay in the fight.

When you sit back and think of all the stuff you dealt with; then think about all the stuff God has brought you through, you can't help but to be grateful that your living another day. As each day is not promise, but one thing is sure; the rain falls on everyone.

As you come to a place of knowing for yourself, then and only then can you be assured that God is real in your life. Even through the toughest times when life didn't make a bit of sense and it seems as if the whole world is against you. You wonder how you were going to make it— yet by divine power— you made it through. Be grateful.

When you sit back and think through the bad choices you made, and how your life was spared. You can't help, but to be thankful that your still here today, getting a chance to get it right. How much more must you see that God is for you and will do what is necessary to get you to understand that all things, whether good or bad works for your good.

When will you see that the best plan in life is the one that the Heavenly Father has for you? His love is pure love that doesn't have stipulation on it, yet we fail to see. Therefore, the next time we want to complain or whine about the hard spots, let's look back at the cross and think of all the suffering Christ endures for us to save us from ourselves!

HOPE FOR TOMORROW

In the daily grind of hope, prayer, and faith; when life turns you upside down smile and say, "I will stay in the race by the grace of God." When the heavy wind blows to and from, and the enemy tries to steal your joy. In this, the unspeakable joy can never be replaced; don't lose faith.

It is when you're down to your last breath and the fight in you wants to fade. Look to the heavens and pray, "Lord, please strengthen and bless me with one more day. I know in you I can win.

Please shield me from the enemy and his friends. Fill me with courage like David to stand firm and not be move by the negative words. I am complete in you when I abide by your Holy Word."

So, every-day I wake-up and smile saying, "Thank you Lord for this day and hope for tomorrow!"

A PROPHET'S CRY

Here I stand waiting and wondering, why this test is harder than before? Did I miss the mark the first go around or is there something I didn't do? Here I stand wiping my eyes, wondering what had happen to make me cry. Did I allow my problems to overwhelm me to the point of frustration?

Father in Heaven, I cry to you not sure as to what I should do. If I move to the right or the left will it free me from stress? Why is it that I am shown everyone's future in full detail except for mine? Am I marked with an unsatisfactory dot? Or am I that significant that the hold the enemy has on me cause me to second-guess who I am?

Lord, it feels like I'm walking this walk alone and the burdens are too heavy to bear. Oh, my soul weeps for release and peace from this desolate place, all I taste is salty tears that continuously cover my face. Wet are my hands and feet with the question rolling in my mind, "Lord, why me?" Yet still pondering how did I bid this misery come to me.

What have I done? What did or didn't I do?

God are you mad at me that you turn your back on me. Or are you testing us to see our loyalty? I'm left with nothing to give, but me with the unknown errors of what causes this isolation from me. It is I, Oh Lord do I cry; please restore to me peace inside. Strength to endure and joy within, holding on to hope for a brighter and better tomorrow!

Hearts, Worship & Inspirations
BEAUTIFUL YOU ARE

Beautiful is the rainbow that comes after the storm.
To remind us of the promise not to flood
earth with rain.

Beautiful is the clear blue skies with bright sunshine.
Make me feel like I am on cloud nine.

Beautiful are the flowers after springtime.
It takes them time to grow,
But when the bud is right and ready to sprout,
the glory of love begins to show.

Beautiful are the birds and the butterflies as
they take care of themselves.
They have been given a task they must address;
it's the circle of life.

Beautiful is the created land, which was made
for you and me.
And with just one touch the Majesty presented
human beings.

Beautiful is the Father whose home is Heavenly.
The love so shared, the Son He bared to save
a sinner's deal,
Came and conquered for us to live eternally.
Indeed, beautiful you are!

Kelamenter M. Smith

WHEN GOD CALLS YOU FAITHFUL

Late night confessions and forgiveness of sin; praying for strength for the unfinished work again. Please fill me with the fruits of your spirit to help me to grow physically and spiritually. Heavenly Father, my life is in your control.

When I was young, I couldn't see why my grandmother and mother prayed the way they did. Now that I am older, I know what praying means to me. If I go throughout one day without talking to you, I'm missing an important component to make my life complete.

The reflection of you is what I most desire, walking in the gospel and making you proud. Cleanse me where impurities have set in. I want to be made whole. Let my Life shine with your light so that others will want to know you.

When my journey has ended and my time on Earth has been long overdue. My goal is to be in the group that do all that we were call to do. I want to be one that you call faithful, "Come home to your Father and my kingdom!"

WHEN GOD GIVES YOU A NEW SONG TO SING

Lately all the songs sung have been sad and alone trying to find that happy place in my home. You search all day long, but no love and no place to call your own; just the empty vessel inside. You hear of others making it through, but you wonder when your time is coming for you to shout with joy too.

I was once told that I would reap the benefits of what I had sown, but how long must I sow to reap a little harvest? All I know is the more I sow, the less I reap. Now where is the benefits from that; don't want to look at another's situation because it's not for me, but often do wonder what's my happy song and when will I be able to sing glad songs.

Lately all the songs sung have put me in a state of stress to depress and not where I'm used to being. I want a new song to sing, but Lord let it come from you. For in you I will find joy and serenity. The love on until that time come I will search for that one song!

LIVING BEYOND SELF: Searching For Meaning

MY GRACE IS STILL SUFFICIENT

As the days draw nearer to its final close and life that used to make sense, doesn't make sense anymore. When your hope is hanging by a string, but you're yet holding on. The Father says... "My grace is still sufficient."

When life's roads seemed to have more bumps and wrong turns, than you can ever imagine, you try to keep your head up and smile through it all. But lately it feels like a waste of energy when the reality is; you want to tell that one how you really feel. The voice says... "My grace is still sufficient."

When the Hellhounds have picked you for their target and no relief has come to you. You wish you could fight back, but not enough strength is left in your tired bones. You pray "Sweet Jesus, I am all alone and my hope is gone." An angelic whisper... "Grace is still sufficient."

In your heart, you want to say, "but Lord, why me?" All those late nights and dreary days, wondering if you're the only one dealing with the heavy tribulation in life. But the grace of God is like a comforter that is wrapped around your soul, bringing peace to your mind.

Yes, I do believe that God's grace is sufficient and that the Father sees my troubles. I am glad to know that my troubles are being worked on and trouble will not last. His grace is great toward me!

GRACE AND MERCY BEYOND MEASURE

It's not happenstance You came to me this way. I was broken, abused, and felt abandoned. You told me to trust You, but I shielded myself within flesh wanting to erase the pain, shame, and bad memories. Yet, You told me You can use it for my gain. Lord, what gain can I receive, when I felt like I was buried in misery?

Words that were spoken had no meaning, so to me what makes your words any different. Give me a chance to show you and let my Holy Spirit console you, I Am the One that can go the distance and show you the plans I have for you.

Therefore, what the enemy meant for evil, I have the authority to turn it around for your good. I'm not at all a magician, so you can throw that thought away I am the One, the Master Builder that one they call the Great I AM.

But Lord God why me, what did I do to deserve this ill-gotten treatment? This was never about you any way; it is all to get back at Me. You were born into this, now you choose how you want to live. I don't want to live like this. Lord, I want to be free. Then what's holding you back to come to me!

"Come to Me, all you who labor and are heavy laden, and I will give you rest. Take My yoke upon you and learn from Me, for I am gentle and lowly in heart, and you will find rest for your souls. For My yoke is easy and My burden is light." (Matthew 11:28-30, NKJV)

SOAK ME IN HEALING WATERS

I came to you because there's no other help I know. I've been living in the land of misery, but I want to go to the land of more than enough. I cried and cried, but still no change, please take this pain from me. Soak me in your healing waters and make my life complete.

Bind the enemy away from me, I want to be close to you. Tell me what needs to be done, and that I will do. I've tried everything, but always failed, now I understand why. I did things without consulting you first and letting your grace abide.

Please renew me rightly inside-out, purge me with your hyssop as my soul screams and shouts. The joy of the Lord is my strength and in Him, I must confide. Life brought many disappointments that made even grown men cry. But it's just a stepping stone to bring forth that gifting inside of you.

Let the Heavenly Father use you and you'll be surprised, he has the best insurance policy for mankind. Put your hope in the Lord as he grants you another day, to be that example of what Christ did.

Live a life full righteousness and not sin, remember Christ died for us so that we may live. Glorify the Lord in all you do. The Creator that brings you life, know that in Him. He gives love without a price!

A PRAYER FROM ME TO YOU

Abba Father, glorious is your works that is before me. Glory to you, almighty and strong in all your greatness, let everyone speak of how great you are. Abba Father, it is because of you we live, move, breathe, and have our very being. There is none like you O` Holy One. You cause the moon, the stars, and the sun to set in due time. You created the sky from land and land from the ocean. You created the animals and the very first man, and then place them on Earth. No one can do what you did and in this, we say "Thank You."

Abba Father, I am interceding for the ones that read this prayer both now and in the future. I pray that you will open their eyes to see the revelation of who you are and that they grab hold to the revelation. I pray that they will walk in the full divine purpose you O` Lord has for them. Abba Father, forgive them, Father forgive us and replenish us with strength, stamina, courage, and faith to endure the journey that is set before us.

Abba Father, touch, heal, and deliver those who have fallen by the wayside and recover the lost that we may minister to them, to draw them by the words of our testimony. Let your light shine through me for the whole world to see You and only You.

My prayer is that you take off the external covering of the world and enclose yourself with the Heavenly Father presence.

Thank you for your loving kindness that you continuously display. Thank you in advance for restoring, forgiveness, deliverance, refreshing spirit, your everlasting love, mercy, and grace! Amen.

LOVE IS

The sweet valley that blooms multiple colors is everywhere. Hearts dancing with joy and eyes with gleam waiting for the love to come to your domain. Peeking through the essence of time, I came just for you.

The unconventional gesture you gave revealed to you the insecurities you have toward me. But I assure you, I have no ulterior motives but to love you bountifully. My love is doing the unexpected and giving my all to make any situation better than what it was.

Love is creating an atmosphere that kisses the very heart and soul of a person. Love is patient, kind, delightful, protective, trustworthy, and strong. Love speaks truthful words and gives encouragement.

The reflection displays a glow that shine throughout, and unreserved joy. From the highest mountains to the lowest valleys, I have loved you. From the very first moment of your existence, I loved you. My love is giving up the best, so that you can have the best. This is how much I love you!

JUST BECAUSE

Here I stand in awe of you, praising and giving thanks to you. Your timing is always perfect no matter what season I'm in, trusting in Him is key. Learning how to solely, depend on you has instilled in me values and strength. The strength that came upon me and power within I'd never known.

You have shown us you in adverse circumstance, but not once have you allowed our foot to dash against the stone. In those gloomy moments, you send rays of sunlight our way to tell us that you see our situation and restructuring things to come our way.

With each sweet dream you give us, we are given hints and tips about the future you want us in.

Thank you for loving us so much to bring the promises to pass. Time and time again you have shown us how much you love us.

Yet you say just because.......I Love You!

STREAMS OF BLESSINGS

Like a flowing river that constantly moves, like the wide rainbow after the storm. There is no end to what the divine has in store for you. Like the cool wind that has no set time, like the seasons that know its place in life.

When the shifting comes and no one truly knows what is going to happen. Yet hoping for miracles, signs, and wonderful wonders to unfold before you. When the morning dew is freshly dropped on a green leaf, no one can really understand the significance of that projection. Just a touch from the Master is what you want to feel.

Yet, praying for streams of blessings to flow your way, for what price have you paid to receive a high return such as this? No abrasive action, no judgmental views are required, just one simple answer will suffice to this question; what do you do when your hope is gone?

Remain in your faith and stand on the Holy Word, always know its work and working for you despite how it feels. Your best interest is in the heart of the Master. The cares and concerns in you are the Master "to go" fuel for the work He does for you.

Just remain true, he wants you anyway to be reunited with him. We ought not to get caught up in the blessings, but in the one that creates them for you. The Master loves you enough to build, design, and open any doors for you, if it His will. The only offering he graciously accepts is that you accept Jesus Christ as your Lord and Savior!

Psalms 88:2 (NKJV) *"Let my prayer come before You; Incline Your ear to my cry."*

Psalms 141:2 (NKJV) *"Let my prayer be set before You as incense...."*

1 Thessalonians 5:16-18 (NKJV) *"Rejoice always, pray without ceasing, in everything give thanks; for this is the will of God in Christ Jesus for you."*

Colossians 4:2-4 (NKJV) *"Continue earnestly in prayer, being vigilant in it with thanksgiving; meanwhile praying also for us, that God would open to us a door for the word, to speak the mystery of Christ, for which I am also in chains, that I may make it manifest, as I ought to speak."*

MY PREFERRED PRAYER

Father God, I take your words, wisdom, and warnings to heart. I am grateful that you invest your precious time into me to show me exactly how much you love me and are concern about me. Father God, I want so desperately to please you, thank you for your mercy and grace. You know me from the inside-out, you know that behind every good intention there are bad intentions as well.

Father God, I'd rather walk under your guidance and directions than any so-called good intentions that may seem right. I surrender my life, my will, my hopes, my dreams, my mind, and my very being to you for the transformation, configuration in me and for me, so that you get the glory out of my life. I can't begin to comprehend the things you plan for me without being renewed and in right standing by you. Renew my mind to de-clutter everything that is not of you, and to take on the mind of Christ. Everything you desire for me to do and to let your will be done.

Father God it is all about you and your plans for our lives, many have fallen by the wayside because of doubt, fear, sin, lack of your wisdom, and knowledge.

Father God let your light so shine upon me that the whole world will see you through me. Stir up the gifting that lies deep within me as you manifest your plans in my life and bring them into the natural. Father God, I want all of you, even when it feels like you're not there; I will still follow hard after you.

Father God, I thank you in advance for every weight lifted, every blessing that you send in my life, every relationship that is bonded through your word and love, every hard lesson, trial, and disappointment. Thank you for not giving up on me when I stayed away.

Thank you for keeping me throughout the years, months, days, and hours. Thank you for protecting us while we slept. Your presence is what we long for and it is there where we find the answers, peace, joy, and gladness. Thank you, Heavenly Father, and Amen!

ON BENDED KNEES

Daily I have come to you but lately it hasn't been the same. The enemy has me in a turmoil whirlwind. It seemed like the caves of chaos was crashing in. I tried to handle it on my own, I thought I was strong enough to carry the load. I thought I could win.

Everyday there was a new issue added on, which made my problems feel ten times stronger. I cried "Lord, I'm sorry I tried to put my two cents in, but I only made things worse for me, I can't do this again. I'm sorry that I've come to you after the huge mess I made, but you are the only one that can correct this and make things straight again."

So, I come to you on bended knees praying that wholeness be renewed. Strengthen me with just your touch and make me feel complete in you. No longer making decisions on my own, I want to be led by you, direct me and speak to me, and that I will do. Where would I be without you? I do not want to know, but just a little talk with Jesus made me feel all right.

Daily I seek you for my daily bread, reading your living word, for my life belongs to you. Cover me with your saving grace in the path for which I take, help me to stay focus because I don't want to stray. Draw me nearer, nearer blessed Lord as I look to you. My feet were walking in the wrong direction, but now led by you.

Fill me with your impeccable power to finish this cross-country race, redeem to me the time I've lost to impact many along the way. Therefore, on bended knees I come seeking you for all things, to finish what was started in me a long time ago!

HELLO HALO

If you can see the weight I bear, the stuff the enemy tries to hold against me. If you could see the weight I bear, the charges the enemy tried to bind me in. If you could only see what tried to hinder me, would you have fled, stayed, or prayed?

I had even arrived at the point where I'm screaming "Hello Halo, can you help me please?" But no answer, no help, it felt as though I was bleeding. Away o' wretched pain, you've kept me in this place far too long for me to hear my name. The deep wound you had me fixed on was more than I can take.

If you could see my scars and the dried tears from the guilt, shame, and pain, would you have cried too? They say we have assigned angels over us, where were mine and why didn't they save me?

Um, Hello Halo could you be a little quicker next time, I'm in a bind, please. These unmarked pains have me feeling as if I'm about to drown. I just need a touch from you to take all my burdens away. Calgon has nothing on you, a touch from the Master's hand will do. Release me, relieve me, Lord please make me whole again.

I'm tired of wasting time on frivolous things; instead of listening to you and my realization is that I NEED YOU!

TOUCHED BY AN ANGEL

In my dream, I hear sweet melodies everywhere. The angels I've seen are tall and I came near the tip of their wings. Golden and bright lights as each angel tends to their assigned people, places, and other things. No one is sitting down but working for the Father.

With each new assignment, with each new birth and with each one returns an angel on duty. Oh, how amazing is it that angels are working for me and are assigned to me. The minute I begin to pray the angels are waiting to hear what I say. They watch, sing, and protect me as I pray.

Oh, how sweet the sound when His name is called. The power in His name signifies that He truly reigns. Not taken lightly nor in vain, the name above all names has shown "How great thou are!"

Such a sweet dream and the peace within, lets me know that I've been touched by an angel. For my mind will never be the same, since my dreams felt like I was in a heaven prelude!

Kelamenter M. Smith

FREE

Abba Father, free me from the pain that hides me from your light. Free me from the dark and dreary nights. Free me to love unconditionally even when the enemy tries to hold my past against me.

Abba Father, free me to walk in the newness of you. I've been washed in his blood, Christ has made me new. Free me to follow your path while others may sit back and laugh. I want you to have total control, being obedient to your word, for Heaven is my goal.

Abba Father, free me to look to you when I fall out of place, help me to dust myself off and learn not to make the same mistakes. Free me from all guilt and shame, when I wanted to hurt those that cursed my name. Free me to love me and to receive love in return, no more hurting and being left alone. Free me to desire your work and will. Free me to trust in your sovereignty; free at last, free at last.

Thank God Almighty I'm free at last; this is my theme I sing from the late Dr. Martin Luther King. Free from bondage and the chains of sin because of God's grace I can make it to the end!

SWEET MELODIES

Sweet is your voice as you whisper my name. Sweeter than any honeycomb or sugar cane. The sweet strings I hear as the angels are singing. Glory in the highest; let all God's people rejoice at his name.

Sweet is your voice as you say, "I Love You." Sweeter than the misty dew after the morning rain. The lovely flute that is played with joy. Oh, what a lovely instrument yet there's many to display a beautiful sound of your glory. However, what is desired, is a pure and humble worship from humanity. A one-on-one relationship that is breath-taking.

Sweet is your voice as you say "Stay." It is sweeter than any song to be sung. Your sweet presence I've always longed for, but after being with you I thirst for more. You are the essence of what to hunger for. I love being with you, you are the one I adore.

Sweet melodies, safe, and secure is what I feel when I'm with you. But when I'm away from your presence I'm lost without a care, lonely, and in despair. I don't want to feel that way again, not ever. So sweet melodies please don't leave, I can go all day singing your sweet name!

LET'S STAY TOGETHER

Lovely are your ways and how you make me feel. Once I'm in your presence all my fears and doubts are blown away. I'm flying high when I'm with you. Not a care in the world, but what more can I do to please you.

Love of my life you bring me joy, an overwhelming feeling that next to you the world can't compare. My love, you are truly the one that embraces me with love lasting throughout eternity. What more can be said about your character, your personality, and your style? Heaven is blessed to have such a wonderful love that makes the whole world smile.

My love, I smile at the very thought of you. So, my love, I propose that this relationship can and will be amazing, so let's stay together you and I. I will do whatever I can to please you and keep that smile in place. I don't ever want to be removed from your grace because I'm in love with you!

SEASONS ALWAY CHANGE

Seasons always change, I Thank God that they do. I do not want to be stuck in one place, as one more season becomes anew. My pain and my struggles is just a season. The best part is I don't have to stay in that same cycle. There is always a refreshing and a renewing as each season comes. May my new season, new levels, and new me, bring glory unto the Father who has always kept and protected me from birth to everlasting.

His Love is Supreme in all things and as the rain comes. I count the many blessings that the Father has given me. As seasons always change, I am yet holding on to promises of God. The Holy Word says, "Jesus Christ is the same yesterday, today, and forever." So, embrace the change and let the work of His spirit take lead.

The Father knows what is best and like a polished jewel; You will be made into a sparkling gem that no tarnish can stain. His craftsmanship is Holy, Royalty, and Anointed, flowing for His plan. We go through changes to see what we are made of, so as autumn comes so does the rain.

But don't get caught up in life's displeasure and pain. Just know that the Heavenly Father has it all in His hands. He is a Miracle Worker, just trust in Him for He is always On Time!

SAVORING THE MOMENTS

With each passing day, with each gentle touch from you, I smile. With a soft and tender kiss across my cheek, I blush. From the moment, I met you, you have taken my breath away. There is no greater feeling than what I am feeling now. With each mellow word spoken and the laughter we share, I am in awe of you.

With each passing moment, I dare not to be without you; wanting every second of the day to be with you, I'm in love. No one can truly understand what goes on between you and me; But an endless adoration that clings from me to you, I am stronger with you.

As the sunlight warms my face and a sweet aroma of grace comes my way, I am grateful. In my mind I'm thinking, "If this is what heaven feels like, I want to go. Take me to a place where there are no dark clouds hovering over the bright sunshine."

A place where it's not just a house, but a place to call home, your kingdom is where I want to belong. So, I learned to savor the moments I spend with you, but I am lost without you.

Kelamenter M. Smith

Forgive me if I took advantage of your time, but you're all I want in my lifetime. There is not a day that goes by when I don't think about you. When I'm with you I feel like I'm on cloud nine.

This is how I feel when I'm with you, an indescribable feeling of peace, love, and joy overflowing in me. It makes me feel like I want to burst with gleam and sing Oh what a feeling!

TALKING TO THE FATHER

Heavenly Father,

Lately it has been hard trying to stay true to you, while all I see is sin, but I do not want to be caught up again in that dead-end whirlwind. I am trying so hard to be my best for you and live right for me to be with you. Nevertheless, at times it seems like I failed in that too or at least that is what the enemy continuously tells me. So, I come to you constantly to hear what You have to say because Your words and your voice is the only thing that matters to me.

Heavenly Father,

Lately it has been rough trying to win souls for You; nowadays no one wants to hear about or witness about the Good News. Every day I hear some people say that it is a waste of time and that You do not hear me. But I tell them I beg to differ and if you all truly knew Him you all would be doing the same, you feel me. Once again, they want to try to pretend as if they do not have issues too. I know I have issues, which is even more reason to come to You.

Thank You Lord for calling me out and removing me from that dead place. I believe if it were not for your mercy and grace, I never would have made it. Moreover, today O' Lord I ask that You please forgive me in all that I say and do. I want to live a life that is pleasing to You. Lord your word says, *"For I know the thoughts that I think toward you, thoughts of peace and not of evil, to give you a future and a hope"* (Jeremiah 29:11 NKJV).

So, Lord, I hope you would give your angels charge over me as I prepare for another day to overcome. Let your guiding light direct my path, be my covering in the midst of a storm. Lord, as I end this prayer yet still in your care, and keep us safe from harm. Please bless this day with the fruits of your Spirit as we, your servants sound the alarm!

A REFLECTION OF YOU

They say mirrors do not lie. However, if that is true then tell me what do you see when the mirror reflects the true you. Do they see a timid little boy or girl wanting to be free?

Or on the other hand, do they see a loving man or woman, who loves one another unconditionally? Wait. Stop and think about it for a moment. If reflection is an idea, an image, an impression, or a representation, we often take for granted that we represent.

What we imitate? Who we imitate? Why we imitate?

If I am to represent a lady, then my walk, my talk, and how I dress should detail that quite well. Projecting some undignified half dressed, without a single moral, and giving it away presale of ones' self. Who's to blame for the imagery game in which we want to play?

Take a step forward and look in the mirror for that reflection is you. Change your thoughts, change your life, and if we are to reflect the attributes of Christ-like. But how can this be in you and me, when the entire world sees their self in the mirror; screaming right back at you saying "Do you see what I see?"

The reply would be "no", while to them it is a joke saying, "Christians are the same and nothings change" from their point of view.

Lord, I do not want to be in that category I truly want to be a reflection of you. So here I stand, bold and tall, do whatever you must do, until they see, know, and believe that I am a living representation of You!

THE FLOW OF PEACE

The sweet smell of lavender in the early morning dew as it caresses the lilies of the valleys. The gentle touch of an Angels' embraces as you quickly, yet slowly go to sleep.

No visions, no dreams, just sweet rest for a new day. The warring is never over, but the guarantee of peace is what we all long for, only one can give it and truly mean it.

The mesmerizing melody of his voice echoes in my heart "I still Love You." I'm embracing those words with all my might and strength. The tranquility of streams of water and a light breeze in the morning can reflect the meek, yet simple things in this life.

The security of your covering has me in a place of rest and relaxation. The calmness in the atmosphere lets me know that the flow of peace is within reach.

I must believe in the One True Source from which it came from to obtain that endless peace. A joy that flows from a divine place that gives us reassurance, my sweet Savior in Heaven!

Kelamenter M. Smith

GRATITUDE

In this topsy-turvy world, many have forgotten how to show gramercy to one another. Why is it that we wait until a holiday to extend love when God has shown His love toward us daily?

Are we that fickle that we wait until there is a crowd to show goodness to be seen doing something. Or are we that capricious that we allow our environment to dictate how we should behave?

Some say that your learned behavior begins at home in private, well if you're a spiritual being would your behavior represent the Heavenly Father. Hmmm...it is a question that may or may not have been answered and may never will be answered.

During this Thanksgiving season, let us not forget the ones that demonstrated their love toward us through out each passing day and year. Showing a kind gesture does not display weakness or being timid, but God requires that of us, so why not do it. Therefore, I am truly grateful for the love that is bestowed upon me every morning. It is even in the Scriptures: "Because of the Lord's faithful love we do not perish, for His mercies never end.

"They are new every morning; great is Your faithfulness" Lamentations 3:22-23 (HCSB).

Thank You Father, for not letting me perish, but growing up in your grace and unfailing love. It is because of you that I live, move, and breathe. I do not want my life to be a pure waste for you, but a pure delight that lives for you. I am in deep gratitude for and because of you.

Thank You!

RESTORE ME O' LORD

Shattered pictures frames against the floor. Stains in the carpet shadowed with pain. Rags soaked and drenched with tears and sweat. Dreading to backtrack our steps from the very first day why didn't I accept you then, Lord forgive me.

Buried in debts, anguish, frustrations, and doubt. Wasted years on you and you weren't even mine. I gave myself to you at a drop of a dime, yet realizing I laid with the enemy. Now broken, saddened, and used, Lord, how can I come back to you this way? I'm ashamed and can't face you.

Dusty clothes from three days ago, with no place to lay my head. Stomach rumbling and longing for a piece of bread. My body wrapped and clothed in pain, wishing I made better choices back then. Now I lay in wait for my funeral to arrive, if you O' Lord do not revive me.

I have nothing left to give, but this piece of life I live and that is not worth much. Screaming out with all my might, Lord, will you help me? I want to be free.

Father God I'm sorry I didn't take heed to your voice nor trust you when you came. I don't want to live this life without you again. I tried it my way and now I'm in a hole, searching for your light. Lord, please restore me and I will not let go. All I need is a new day and a fresh door of opportunity!

A NEW

The rain pounding upon my head, mini pearls of water glide down my face. Looking, trying to adjust my eyes, but the view seems farther and farther away. Trying to shift gears, but the stiffness will not let me move. Not wanting to be limited to just my circumstance.

Nevertheless, if given one more chance I'm plunging forward. Refusing to go back to familiarity, those days are long gone. I declare I am putting the old self to rest and redress in the spirit of refresh.

New clothes won't do it, nor will a new hairdo, but it's all from the inside-out the new me through a system of purity. Everything I thought I knew is gone out the door, now filled with you and your amazing grace.

Never had I felt love this way, it's still new to me, but I want it, I need it and nothing else will do. You have set the standard of what is expected of me and I am longing to do it. I'm glad feelings are neither required nor are any skills, but you O' Lord have supplied all my needs; not some, not one, but all my needs, so I'm indebted to you!

THE FLOW

Tears is an action from one's soul, every time one tear drops, it tells a story. And every time the story is told, you see and read memories unfolding. So, make sure the flow is slow and not painfully long. I tried closing my eyes to my present situation and realized only the Heavenly Father can change all things.

My mind constantly repeats that statement, every time my flesh looks at the problem and not toward God. But, then I am left saying, "Now what, what do I do now?" Do not doubt, it only adds to the problem and gives no rest. God has everything under control.

I reach out to you oh, Lord on my bended knees. Please help me get through this storm, for I need thee. Daily seeking you and chasing you so that I can be near you. Lord, teach me how to leave all my cares and concerns over to you. Even though I may say I leave it, but do not do it.

Victory is what I want over every area in my life even those hidden areas I tried to forget about. Restore me Oh Lord God in You, by You, and for You. Every moment I am not in your presence, I am lost without you.

LIVING BEYOND SELF: Searching For Meaning

My very being could not come into existence without your touch and your breath of life. I am like a ship with no sail just wandering about. Never knew such a love so grand than the love You have for me. So, I thank you Lord for strengthening me in my weakest moments!

CROSSING JORDAN

The water is too deep, too cold to get in. The feeling of giving up has become my friend. Streams of water running down my face, asking myself why I came this way. The pain of struggles has enclosed upon me.

Looking for help in others not like you, what was I to do? They got me all twisted around looking like a class clown. I fail, I'm sorry. It's no fun walking in pain, but I'd rather be alone than in a sad group with guilt and shame; those types of clothes I can't fit anyway.

Clothed me with your presence and fill me with love to model for you what the whole world needs to see; an example of what they should be. I am better and living better when I'm with you. When out of your will I am like a lost sheep trying to cross the river Jordan with no help to meet my needs, such an empty feeling, alone, and in despair.

I've been in that dark place and I don't want to go back there. I can't see my way through, but your light gives me a wider brighter view. Now I see that crossing Jordan is not that deep when my trust and faith is in You!

LOVE WITHOUT COST

A man of an average stature, very common to some, with a normal occupation to gain skills until further notice. Quite familiar with hands-on training, no doubt there, this man was known by his family surname. But who is he, really?

No one really knew, just someone into wood and nails, I suppose. A woodsman...no a carpenter... yes. It was the family business and helped pave the way for greater works were stored. The final call, now the real work has begun and many were astounded at the ex-carpenter doing all these astonishing works.

Everyone wondering, "Who is this man that came from Joseph and Mary?" "Is He a magician with hidden secrets to tell? Or is he a pretender that knows the Scriptures very well?" He came and uprooted everything they thought they knew. He dismantled the tables and cleaned out the house. A pure place to worship is what He made it about for the rest of the days. Holy, Holy, Holy is the lamb our sacrifice, yet it was still unseen.

He gave hope, life, and love; yet through it all He prayed; "Lord, not my will, but your will be done." He knew the high price it cost and why the debts must be paid. But he did it anyway, with no murmuring or complaining.

The greatest love that could never compare to anything the world may try to offer you, is a love worth dying for. Many people have taken their loved one for granted, thinking they will be okay.

But how can anyone seize the amount of love to give, when the offering was stretched out wide for everyone to see just how much we are loved. A love without a cost, he gave his life for the entire world. This is a love worth fighting for, a true love story!

BEAUTIFUL WINGS

In Loving Memory of Laverne McCurtis

*Y*ou came and touched the earth before I got to know you, already paving the way. You were engaging in lives with a sense of humor, a magnetic personality, and love.

Your personality is one-of-a kind that can never be duplicated or replaced. But to have known you was a wonderful journey and I am grateful for the time.

Beautiful within and out, you seem to bring every situation from gloom to light. Your humorous ways left everyone asking, if you were a comedian in your previous life. You care so much for others well-being that you have always initiated the first move. From making calls to negotiating assignments and watching it flow.

We are appreciative of all the fond memories and the laughter we shared. Fighting back the tears and holding on to the "Remember when" that put smiles upon our faces. The day you were called home, I know the sound of rejoicing rung all over Heaven, another one has returned home to receive her beautiful wings.

Kelamenter M. Smith

As with each passing day, we too hope to reunite in the Heavenly courts rejoicing as well. But until then, just know that you will be missed and loved. We thank the Heavenly Father for the fantastic time with her and warm-hearted reflections. We will meet again to see more wings that are beautiful and hear the angels sing!

LIVING BEYOND SELF: Searching For Meaning

IF I CLOSE MY EYES

If I close my eyes and think of you, would you appear?

If I close my eyes and say your name out loud,
you would come see me?

If I close my eyes and count to five,
would you be there?

If I close my eyes and sing the alphabet song,
would you stand by me?

If I close my eyes and turn around three times,
would you catch me?

If I close my eyes, break down and cry,
would you console me?

If I close my eyes and opened them again,
but could not see, would you help me?

~

I would be there for you, if the tables were turned.

I would come see you, console you, and stand by you.

Kelamenter M. Smith

I would dine with you, cry with you, and hold your hands.

I would catch you, cradle you, and carry you too.

∼

Again, I would be there for you because I care for you, deep down in my heart. But it's hard to truly see you with that dark mask on. Remove the mask and let me see the real deal, I promise you there will be no shame. I just want to love the all-natural You!

LIVING BEYOND SELF: Searching For Meaning

IN PURSUIT OF MY FIRST LOVE

The cold steel bars that caged my heart from you, made me realize how much I need you. The hollowness that has engulfed me, forbid me to see your beauty and majestic works. Nonetheless, for whatever reason I'm still here.

Wait, hold up I'm still in the race. Shifting in this process is challenging, but I can't stop. I won't stop. Your love for me is far greater than I can ever imagine, Even in my darkened dreams you still pursued me.

I must break free from the delusion of you not wanting me, when it is relevant that you do. Now I must change my perspective and the way I go after you.

Clear my mind of all the ways and refresh me with you. Let this new revelation move me higher in elevation of getting closer to you. Forgetting those things, which is behind and pressing hard in pursuit of my first love, which is you!

Kelamenter M. Smith

BY THE WAY...I LOVE YOU

In Loving Memory of Bishop Steven Bennett

Never missing a beat, you walk in so proud, but not to the point that it would get you caught up. You were proud to be who you are. The impact that you had on many lives will show you who truly loves you. You've had the most memorable moments that were never captured. Your style, your grace and your personality made it so easy to love you. You even owned up to your flaws, which made Your integrity shine even more.

The heart of giving and the love you share was embedded in your DNA, not to mention your sense of humor and your smile. We're reminded that big things can come in small packages. Well you made sure of that, you lived life big and wanted us to do the same. You were a man after God's own heart.

You are a Big Deal and we want you to know that no matter what we do, God will get the glory. Your fire and zeal for God is ineffable, there is no one like you. You brought joy, laughter, tears, and most of all compassion.

Kelamenter M. Smith

In Matthew 7:16a *"You will know them by their fruits"* (NKJV). Also in Luke 12:48b *"For everyone to whom much is given, from him much will be required"* (NKJV).

You produced much fruit and your fruits continue to grow. We will not let your fruits wither and die. We're determined to rise in our destiny. Thank you for 25 years of stewardship!

We love you and we miss you!

WHY I SMILE

I don't know what the future holds, but I know who holds my future. He has brought me through many things good and bad, seen and unseen; therefore, I smile.

The enemy traps and snares that were set up for me did not prosper. Even when my feet skid across troubled waters and dodged fire darts. I'm still standing, this is why I smile.

The agape love given to me with unmerited favor, even though I was unworthy to receive it. The Father of Heaven still loved me and watched over me. This is why I smile.

Selected to be His own and raised to praise the King upon the throne. From darkness to light You died to make things right. Now I stand sharing my part of a faith filled journey.

I smile at the very thought of You and what you brought me through, there was absolutely no way I could have made it without You. I take comfort in knowing that despite my faults You will guide, speak, and lead me in the right direction. As I continue to follow hard after you I will always have a reason to smile!

Letters of Strength

<u>In the time of trouble, I know You</u>
<u>are with me. Because of you, I have</u>
<u>strength to overcome the challenges</u>
_____
_____
_____

He gives power to the weak, And to those who have no might He increases strength.

Isaiah 40:29

Kelamenter M. Smith

DEAR FRIEND

Dear Friend,

I wanted to talk to you today, but the pain and misery in my life makes it hard to bear. My tears have been my pillow and I am at my wit's end. Who can I turn to that would ease my sorrow and life's disappointments with no hope for tomorrow? My only Friend in whom I can truly confide in, but can you hear me? I could truly need your help; my back is up against the wall and I'm trying not to stress myself out.

Please help me understand the madness that I'm in. I tried to reach out to others, but no one can do what you can. Everything seems to make no sense to me and I'm so confused. I mean the weight of this load is heavy and my heart is shattering.

Hello Friend, I wish that you were near, I could use a fervent prayer right now. I know I promised to contact you until things were clear, but it has gotten worse. Please keep me in prayer and agree with me, that I make it through the storm.

May God keep me when I lost heart and even searched outside of Him, when I should have kept my eyes on Him. Thank you, friend for your time and letting me vent for a while and sending me a prayer to help me in my time of need.

Signed,

Your Dearest Friend

RE: DEAR FRIEND

Dear Friend,

I prayed for you today. I prayed that your day was one that was Godly driven and directed under the Holy Spirit. I prayed that the issues of life you have been praying over will be answered according to God's will. My concern about you is taken from the company you kept for so long that they have become your validation support group, when in fact they have no desire for you to grow in wholeness.

I prayed for you today. I prayed that the love God has for you will envelope you so close and so tightly that you can't move without feeling His presence. I prayed that you release every situation unto Him that you thought you could handle, but couldn't. I prayed you release even the situation you can handle, however using Godly wisdom in all things is best.

I want you to know my dearest friend, I am constantly praying for you. Therefore, if there is something that you don't or can't share with me, I'm putting that in prayer as well. I prayed that the Heavenly Father will provide you the answers and comfort you need for that secret prayer.

Kelamenter M. Smith

As I close in prayer, just know that you are in my life for a reason and if God permitted that you stay longer it's for a lifetime. May the Father richly dwell in your surroundings that everything that was dry, the Father brings life. It's because of the Father that we have life and move. Moreover, I prayed that you will seek Him first and know that I'm still praying for you.

Signed with Love, From One Friend to Another

Sincerely Yours

SINCERELY YOURS

Hello My Love,

I want you to be the first to know although we had many good times, but I'm afraid that I must go. It was good to be with you and even though I did things to make you mad. Now I wish I could take them all back to see your smiling face again.

Hello, my sweet, I'm remembering more and more, remember that I love you anyway. The way you laugh, the way you smile, the tears we shed, and the memories we shared. I cannot say that those were the good olé days because I have changed my life completely.

The thrills, the chills, and all the crazy stuff we used to do, they no longer excite me now the way they use to. Party here, party there, I had it going on, but it messed me up and left me feeling wore down. So no longer afraid to say goodbye, this is real from me to you. It's time I change direction and live my life anew. So goodbye, so long, and know that it's been fun, but things have changed since that day. I'm no longer the old man. Do not look for me in the past I no longer live there. I bid you farewell as I travel into my destiny looking at the best of me.

Sincerely Yours,

The New Me

Kelamenter M. Smith

YOURS TRULY

Dear Child,

First, I want you to know that I do love you and have your best interests at heart. You are a precious jewel and a delicate flower that shines in its season, and blooms where it's planted. When I created you, I put my very best work in you for my plan and purpose. You are part of a royal bloodline and there is nothing more satisfying, than to see you walking in the divine gift I placed in you.

My child, I know that growing in such an unholy world is hard, but know that you have a family that loves and supports you in the process. Now that you have move from milk to solid food, know that the adversary is watching and lurking about to destroy all that is good. You are equipped with the very finest tools and resources possible because nothing is impossible with ME.

I am constantly working on your behalf, so believe me when I say, "I got you in my hands, just trust me." Now there is more to be done and I see that you have inspired others to come to me, very good. I know that you think this blessing is the "Big One", but that is small compared to what I have in store for you. So, enjoy it and know that it is only the beginning.

Remember to be watchful, for the enemy is roaming swiftly destroying your brothers and sisters in the faith. Be mindful to keep them and yourself prayed up, it is neither in vain nor the work that is done for me. I am always watching and working for the good of those that love me.

Signed,

Yours Truly

Just1Call@Heaven.GOD

From: Just1Call@Heaven.GOD

To: poetksmith@xxxxx.com

Subject: Why Don't You Trust Me

Hello Love,

I have chosen you for my divine plan and purpose. I desire to give you so much and yet I ponder on the fact that you don't trust me. What more must I do to prove to you that I can be trusted? Haven't I done enough to show you how much I love you and want you to be with me?

Didn't I protect you from the break-ins, even though our relationship was strained? On the other hand, what about the time I protected you from being robbed and countless of other incidents, I sent my angels to guard you and your family.

I need you to understand that when I speak a thing, it will not return to Me void. When I said "Follow Me" and everything else will fall into place — I meant that. When I said I got your household in My Hands — I meant that. EVERYTHING WILL FALL INTO PLACE (TRUST ME).

I know you've been hurt, abused, mistreated, etc., but I got you still in the palms of my hands. It's all working together for your good and my definition of "good" is different from your definition of "good." When I do bless you, it will not be one specific thing or area. But it will come in like a flood with mighty rushing waters. I have not forgotten you nor will I forsake you.

Now before replying, take time to think about all I have done and said to you and then I will know by your response. However, in the meantime try fasting and meditating over it, to get full clarity of the matter because trust is a factor.

Signed Yours Truly,

Master of Creation

DIARY OF A MISCARRIAGE

(You Never Know the True Value Until It's Gone)

Dear Diary,

I need someone to talk to so I'm writing to you. This day feels uneasy, strange, and I wasn't feeling good at all. Therefore, I stayed mostly to myself, but still something wasn't right within me. I know, I know, I tried saying my prayers but my body wasn't in any physical shape to pray. My head was hurting, running a fever, and my throat felt raw. I didn't know what was wrong with me, my whole body was sore, achy, and in much pain. I stayed curled up in my bed, hoping for some relief. I cried out unto the Lord because the pain was too much to bear. I've missed so much today being trap in the house.

After several hours of unbearable pain, it happened, but why, why me. Why am I going through this? I thought I was on the right track. I thought I was ready for it, but I was wrong. What I lost has changed my entire life and I'm left with an emptiness inside. My smile was turn into a frown in an instant. My dearest has died before its due time and I don't know why.

Dear Diary,

Was it I or was it too soon? Why does it hurt so badly? Oh Diary, I feel awful inside. I think I'm going to just stay in my bed until this hurt subsides. There were no warning signs or nothing. I'm so confused, lost, and dismayed at this tragedy. Even still, it seems like the weight of the pain is still lingering in my mind. I must try to move on and look at it as if it wasn't the right time. But that voice keeps telling me, I'm not wrong. Ok Diary, I have to go and talk to my Father now.

Dear Diary,

Sorry I had left in a hurry, but I needed my Daddy. Well, I was reminded of my true purpose for which I was sent. I lost it, I couldn't deny it, even if I wanted too. I can't believe I had a miscarriage. What was I thinking? As hard as it was, I am given another chance to give birth to the purpose and gifting that is within me by my Heavenly Father. I let fear, doubt, frustration, envy, hatred, and every form of contamination take hold of me, which caused me to miscarry. Now I know and it's not happening again, I'm better now. I'm ready for whatever the Father has for me to do. I will do it to the best of my abilities.

Perseverance

Let perseverance finish its work so that you may be mature and complete, not lacking anything.
                                        James 1:4, NIV

Perseverance

BUILDING A BETTER YOU

Look in the mirror and see the real you, not the pretend you.

Open up to the one who has all cleansing power to take away the deep dark stains.

No man-made cleanser can do it;

No expensive products can do it either.

But the great I AM can get beyond the roots and bring total healing.

So, don't think that you're too far in, that you can't be saved.

When Jesus defeated Hell and came back from the grave.

He can do anything even build a better you for the Kingdom, if He chose too!

Kelamenter M. Smith

PLAGUED BY DISGRACE

Since that day my life has changed, it was hard to trust anyone again because of that secret pain. It ruined me deep inside, the pain yet remains, even though you promised not to do it again. But you came even more powerful and a broken vessel I became. Not once, nor twice, too many times yet I remain.

How could I have been so blind and not see the real you behind those deceiving eyes? When you said, "I will never hurt you." But to my surprise, I was left bruised, broken, and full of tear stained black eyes.

One too many times I let you control me, now you no longer hold me. But I found a real love who wants to console me. He wants to erase the pain that runs deep to my soul, But because of fear I hid my face, thinking I was plagued by disgrace.

No longer feeling the way, I use to feel, but now tainted fits the bill. He pleads with me that I am not that man. If you just take one step, I'll show you who I AM.

Perseverance

The one that can heal all kinds of wounds,
if you let me in I want to heal yours too.

I come not to harm you, but to make you whole again
just so you'll know I'm no ordinary Man.

I want you to trust in me and take my hand;

I promise to ease your fears, the guilt, and the shame.

I will show you how to live again.

Living a life that is happy and free, just take one step
and put your faith in Me!

BEYOND REASON: "PRAY TIL IT COME"

I close my eyes and say, "when will my time come, is it today, tomorrow, or any day now?" What purpose do I have to keep hope alive when change has not come?

What do I say to that child, as they look you in the eyes? Do I say, "Baby, I'm sorry, but hope and prayer didn't help us today?" Do I turn aside to get quick money? On the other hand, do I just say that "whatever comes my way, if I live, I live, if I die, oh well?"

I close my eyes and say "when will my time come, when will it meet me, for I do not know what tomorrow will bring. I can't reason with logic, should I just accept my doom?" My purpose is beyond reason; I'm going to pray 'til it comes'.

No matter what the strong wind brings, I'm going to fight for what's right until my good days come in. I can't look back I must move full speed ahead.

The enemy is on my track trying to make me move five steps back into the muddy clay. I'm on my way to Hallelujah Lane and regain the joy I once had, there is no surprise; the lover of my soul was there to make me glad!

REFLECTIVE MEMORIES

Never reflect on past mistakes too long, it only brings about depression and bitterness. Tell the enemy that you will not go down that road with him.

Never let anyone take you to the path of destruction. Who needs help messing up his or her own life? Never say never, if it can happen to Israel it can happen to you as well, your life is never untouchable for the Almighty to take control.

Take a long hard look at your life and remember who kept you from danger seen and unseen, it is the Almighty that kept you this long. Praise Him as you enter a new year. Be grateful for another year added to your life. Who knows when their number will be called?

Let go of all envy, hatred, and strife; it causes stress on the heart. Live happy and be well. The promise will come and be plant in your life, the word never goes unfulfilled it just changes direction.

Thinking back, I'm glad to say,

> "The Heavenly Father kept me to this day."

My life is better with Him as each step I take.

He understands I am bound to make mistakes,
but his grace and mercy saved me.

Reflection can do you wonders if you first
admit to yourself, confess and connect to the
'True One' that made life possible!

HELLO OPERATOR

Me: Hello operator, I've been trying to make an emergency call, but can't connect to the line. Can you help me?

Operator: ....

Me: Hello.... hello. Please help me if you can, I need to get through the line as fast as I can. Will you help me?

Operator: ....

How would you feel if God didn't answer at all when we call? What would we do or who else can we call on? The enemy will have us going in circles only causing us to fall into a deeper ditch than before. We would be left saying "Help, I've fallen and I can't get up." The only One that can dig deep and pull us out is the Almighty. The enemy has no power over you unless you give it to him.

Me: Hello again……Hello Operator. I dialed the number and it said that this number is no longer in service. How can that be when I just dialed it yesterday?

Me: Can you please help me dial the number? I can't get through and I need to make this call badly.

Operator: ....

When life has stirred up trouble and you're trying to get help out of it. Isn't it just like us to need help when we can't get out of the mess we made ourselves?

What if God wasn't there?

What if God decided to say, "I'm done with you, but I won't let you die?"

Who needs to be washed in the blood of Christ?

Every-day we should be saying, "Lord, I need you to guide me through this day because I cannot make it on my own." Change me for the better and affect the lives of others. I want to become that Godly example of a righteous child, that man or woman of God.

See me beyond my appearance and reach the inner me, you'll be surprised by the awesomeness inside; and the divine glow that has resided in that sacred place — it's your being. Your life has purpose as does mine, but reaching your full potential is the obstacle in which the rough and rugged mountains made it hard to climb.

I AM MORE THAN A CONQUEROR!!!!

MOVING FORWARD

Forgetting the past, reaching for higher heights, I'm going to rise beyond my circumstances. I dare to stand firm. Past mistakes are my stepping stones for making the right choices to a better me. I will not accept defeat as my final round, there's more in me to be unleashed. I am a victor in Christ!

New clothes, new direction, new mind-set, and a renew spirit man. This is all divine and not man-made, only God can change me. Forgiveness of sins has cleared the way, now I know I have to live better, do better. I'm saved for another day, despite what I look like to you. My Creator sees something greater in me, now I'm working to make it a reality.

Greater is he in me, than He that is in the world. Transformation has been my added equipment toward success. If I don't allow it to function, it won't work right or progress properly. As I stand here to see how far I came, I am grateful for the battles I had won. I know that it was not by my strength, but by the divine power of three that rescued me.

Now I am able to move freely understanding that it is the Holy Spirit leading me. I can boldly say this was the best decision made, for without Christ my life would be meaningless, empty, and void. Yet had I'd listen sooner I would be in position already, but you live and you learn. Therefore, I will not drag on the past, but what's ahead, my future destiny. So, goodbye old habits, hello new dreams, it's good to finally be where I'm supposed to be. I'm walking in my divine purpose for it was God's plan for me!

THE BATTLE

The smoldering smell that could kill a million flies. You are wrapped in exhaustion like a thermal undergarment. Your body ejects more water than it can retain. The back of your throat mimics the rough edges of sandpaper.

Your eyes are dim and red from the streams of flowing water. Your knees buckle more as you scream out in agony. You cannot get another word out as your vocal cords limit its movement, barely making it as your arms gives way from the prayer position.

You had to ask, "How long have I been in this battle?" wondering if your prayers have been heard. My God, my God will replenish me for another day, I'm just waiting until that glorious day and the battle will be over. But, until then I will continue to fight to keep my flesh under subjection and keep my spiritual walk right!

COUNTERFEIT

I see the faultiness you try to hide. I see the true you in disguise. I see the sneakiness you try to wear with your sleek smooth tongue yet telling me to beware. I see the cunningness you wear so dear. I see the dark waves in which you appear. However, to your surprise there is a stronger and brighter one that lives within.

The Holy Spirit in whom I confide, holds me close and the one I adore. Because my super hero sent him to me I must be special to him, you see. All the way from what used to be, was me until I met the man who died for me. He came, he conquered, and he could not be defeated. He restored me once again.

I'm no longer afraid of man, but the Heavenly Father that has all power to command. You are just a counterfeit, a has-been, a want-a-be, and a pretender that wants to be God. You can't compare to my Almighty God. You will not nor never be like the Most High.

You even deceive yourself with your sinful pride, looking at yourself as the One True God. Get away from me with your counterfeit behind. You have no place, no power, and no plan, you're just a mocker playing with the lives of humans. Yet thinking you will win; however, in the end. Christ my Lord will still reign!

TREADING THE TRENCHES

It's like walking through those hard dark valleys and you cannot see your way through. It's like a hard season where everything is against you and you're wondering what you have done to cause this chaos to occur.

Believe me, we all have experienced those times in our lives, some experience it more often than others do. In these bleak seasons in our lives, we seem to find no comfort from anywhere.

It's like a dry season where nothing is growing and nothing is producing. It feels like a fruitless life, no seeds to grow more fruit, not anything. We can't help but to pray "Lord, if it's your will please pass this cup from me; Not my will but your will be done."

However, the fact remains we must all bear the burden or aftermath of the cross. Now the question is "Are you mad enough at the enemies' plot to kill, steal, and destroy the very essence of life that Jesus died to save?"

"For God so loved the world that He gave His Only Begotten Son that whosoever believeth in Him should not perish, but have eternal life" John 3:16 (KJV).

Will you believe in Him for your victory? Will you trust in the walk that Jesus took to give us examples of how to live? Will you stay in the fight long enough to hear "Well done my good and faithful servant?"

Will you choose life and not death? "Choose you this day whom you will serve," the prophet said. How long will you go on and deny the Creator the accolades that are beyond deserved?

Time and time again, the small victories God gave wasn't enough to say, "I'll praise You." The heavy weight of the burdens of this world feels like a ton of bricks upon my shoulders. Oftentimes I sit wondering if the Father sees the pain I'm in and why am I here.

Nevertheless, I know the Father see all, I just want this season to disappear. All I can do is pray for strength to get through this and for whatever reason it was place upon me, learn from it and move on. Trust in the Master and his plan for you. I keep telling myself, this too shall pass. Looking to come out on top!

WORK ON ME

The pain, the misery has changed the inner me. No peace, no rest, just tired, and stressed out. No joy more sorrow is all I seem to bear, wishing to build a newer me, but no one really cares. As tears stained my pillow, every day trying to keep my head afloat, wanting the pain to go away.

Isolation is what I feel when I don't hear from you. Wondering if you truly see the hell I'm going through. Sleepless nights, I've tossed and turned laying there wondering why. I've tried to push pass the hurt, but sometimes it comes back ten times stronger not knowing how.

Dark days and long cold nights, pondering where my God is. Has he forsaken me and given up on me? What is it about me that get treated this way I just want to know? Is there such awesomeness that the enemy doesn't want exposed?

I've cried and cried, but still no change has come. I wanted to say what's the use anyway, but that's not me. I know your name and the power you boldly hold. So, I pray for more courage and strength to do your will. I find that even when I'm not at my best your love embraces me still.

Therefore, I don't have to cry no more or look sad and gloomy, just reading your word and the promises will unfold for me at the appointed time. I have to trust in the Father and His plan for me, knowing everything will work out fine. In all the things I had to endure I will not give up hope.

I will remain in your word until my breakthrough comes. Let the work you have in me be completed by you. I will not let go until you bless me Lord!

BELOVED

Dear Love: How are you today? I'm sorry I missed your call. You seemed to have had a lot to say. There are ten messages from you in just one day.

Hello Beloved: I see you're not home. I wanted to talk to you about what went wrong. You said you would be there when I needed you, but now you're not home.

Hello, it is I again, in case you missed my message. I needed to talk to you, but you didn't answer my call. Ok love, now I'm concerned, this makes my third message and you still have not returned my call. Is there something I did wrong? Are you upset about something? Why you are not home? Ok, I will check back later.

Hi Beloved it is now forty-five minutes after the hour and your still not fazed. What did I do today to make you stay away? I need to hear your voice I had a rough day. All I could do is sit, cry, and pray, please don't forget me. I need you right away to comfort and console me while I sleep the pain away.

Now what would our reaction be if we called and called on Jesus and he did not appear. Would we fall back into our sinful ways? Or would we wait around for Him to come? Since He is our beloved and bids us to stay, lets' look to Him that saves by grace!

LIVING BEYOND SELF: Searching For Meaning

AROUND THE TOWN

Bright lights, busy streets
>People coming and going in a hurry.

>Walking here, walking there, cars speeding around to nowhere.

>Do they see or are they blind by their own agenda and time?

>Hurry up time is wasting away in hope that you will get in line, but don't be late.

>Bright lights, busy streets

>People moving but not to your beat.

>They don't realize that they're missing out on something important and valuable to them.

Life is too short to let this slip away, don't let this life or the work disappear. You make time to praise me when it is on your agenda, but what will you do when your time has ended.

Kelamenter M. Smith

You came to me when your situation was bad and when there was too much turmoil for you to handle. You cried and prayed, "Please take the pain away." Now that things are good, you don't want me to stay.

How long will you allow the world to dictate your moves? Are you aware of the path and the swing of their grove? They don't care about your stand for what's right, all they want is to party all night. Therefore, beware of what is going on around the town. You don't want to get caught up with your guard down.

> Bright lights, busy streets
>
> People coming and going in a hurry.
>
> Walking here, walking there; cars speeding
>
> around town to nowhere.
>
> Can't they read between the lines?
>
> In the news people dying at a drop of a dime.
>
> Time will not stand still while you seek
>
> your own selfish gains and thrills.

When will you learn that everything will not go back to the way it used to be, the Day of Judgment is coming soon. The choices you make can determine your fate whether bad or good. The choice is yours!

BY THE WAY

It is clear to me how you feel, it saddens my heart
to hear you say
You have never felt the same way
So now it's over, farewell.

When were you going to tell me this?
Or are you just that coldhearted to love me
than leave me
And keep me hanging by a string.

So, tell me this and I'll be done
Were you going to kiss and run?
Seeing how your hidden agenda
became clear to me,
Wondering if this was your plan
since the beginning.

All the more it was fun while it lasted
Yet still stunned by what you did.
Leaving me vulnerable and drained
of loving anyone again.
Next time will be better for me
And by the way I'm better off without you!

TO SIR, WITH LOVE

Hello sir, I've missed you today. I was wondering why you have not returned my call. Lately, it seems that you're far away from me, but tell me what I can do for you to return back to my presence. I miss you!

Is it another person that swayed you to leave me? Or was it I that cause this relationship to cease? Please inform me so that my decision made will be true. I want you back, please come back to me.

Hello, my love, I see that you need me now, but it wasn't me that had left, it was you. I stood waiting for you to come to me, but instead you went in the opposite direction. Thinking that the grass was greener on the other side.

How surprised you must have felt when the talk you had made things seem real. Only to see the reality of it, he had you fooled, poor you. I tried to warn you more than twice, but you thought he was just being nice.

Now things are discombobulated, you want me to straighten it all out right away. You want us to go back to the way it used to be, but the fact is you never really wanted me for me.

Sorry my love I had to let you see, he was never really on your side with his misleading ways to help you stray. I know that at first you couldn't see, but now your eyes are fully open to the real truth that of which I always speak.

There was never another person, it's always been about me and you and how our relationship grew. But in order to rekindle the flame with me, you must remain true and stay in love that drew me to you!

IN GOD WE TRUST

We say we love you and give you praise, but in the end do we trust you? Or is it when a football team wins the Super Bowl and give thanks to God. When rappers use the same lips to swear and degrade, but later give thanks to God for winning a Golden Globe Award.

In a world full of uncertainty, while the poor get poorer and the rich get richer. How can we say I trust you, yet live a lie? No one knows or really understands what it means to trust God in every area of their lives until they surrender all to him.

Yet we have taken advantage of the phrase "In God we Trust." When the reality is, it's everything else, but God that we trust. Have we disappointed the Almighty with lip service and misguided deeds? Yet we're always expecting Him to come immediately when we call upon Him.

Who are we that we can expect such service when we barely serve the Father the right way? We endanger our lives daily when we serve our own purpose and goals dismissing the True Almighty plan. How much longer are we going to lie in wait not knowing where do we exactly go when the time has come?

Arise, Arise I say, before it's too late; get yourself right before the Judgment day. As you can see, time waits for no one, while more dark days have come to sweep us away. I don't want to be left wondering why, I didn't choose you today!

DON'T FORGET THE BACON

It started early this morning as I was awakened by your gentle touch. My heart was singing with joy as your peace embraced me. As I sat to listen to you, I'm in awe of what was revealed to me. Spending time with you is a blessed moment that I treasure dearly.

Over a couple strips of bacon, I had to ponder what life would have been like if I took one more bad advice? I'm glad that I listened to you or else my dreams would have been cut short the moment I left you.

Be grateful for every new day and always pray, prayer still works. I was in bad shape, but your love, mercy, and grace saved me. I've made plenty of mistakes and some with the high cost I've paid. But the cost cannot compare to the cross you bear and the cruel action that they display.

I'm glad that you didn't turn away from me nor led me away. I'm glad you love me so much that you spared me yet again. I vow to do what's right at any cost as long as I'm with you. You showed me there's no greater love than the love the Father has for me!

HOLD FAST TO YOUR DREAMS

Hold fast to your dreams. So that they won't slip away. It's easy to lose track of them, when the enemy is at bay.

Hold fast to the word of truth. Know that everything in it applies today use it as a reference guide to help you make it through. Apply the word to your life and believe Jesus is the way.

Hold fast and don't let go the Heavenly Father sees, hears, and know. The pain and struggle that his children are going through on this Earth But in the end, we overcome through our Good Shepherd and Faithful Friend.

Your life is God's canvas to create a beautiful picture. Once that work is complete you will see, how wonderful your life truly came to be. So, hold fast to your dreams, trust in the True Almighty King. Believe and abide in him and know that his kingdom reigns forever on Earth and in Heaven!

PAIN KNOWS NO NAME

This adversity that is like a thief that comes to rob, to kill, and to destroy the very essence we call Life. It knows no name. This animosity that is used against me like a knife that cuts so deep, the wound to my heart needs more time to heal.

The aggressor is prowling like a roaring lion looking for some helpless soul to overthrow and rule over them, to distribute this anguish it feels inside. The plan is to annihilate humankind. The atheist looking and laughing while such atrocities enfold the cities with gloom. Who can stand such a burden, buried before the throne?

How can we say we love one another when all we do is bring destruction by the very thing we use to speak to life? Like a double-edged sword, my words will be judged according to what is right.

So, I tell you this straight from the heart, how you treat one another will set apart the rulings of blessings and curses. You will see the agitator brings no mercy, but he only brings pain that knows no name along with misery!

LET MY WORK SPEAK FOR ME

All I do, can be said by my deeds. I don't have to boast or gloat, my work is all I need to speak for me. When I hear those that try to make themselves more than what they appear. I smile to myself and say, "My work is all I need to speak for me."

When accolades are given, and I'm left in the cold. My true kudos comes from the Almighty, whose sings my name in Heaven, every time I put a smile on His face: Heaven knows. All I do, can be said by my deeds I don't have to strut my stuff, my work speaks for me.

So, the next time you come boasting and bragging, remember who gave you the power to overcome. Know that in Him we can come as we are, be fixed for a better tomorrow. Therefore, when the flesh wants to walk in vainglory. My spirit by favor must tame it, to tell the Lord's story.

This is why we are to put away all lust after the flesh and seek after the Holy One. It knows the true identity inside of me. So, the work I do is not for me, but that God gets the glory. I'm, but a mere vessel sharing the Holy Story!

HELPING OTHERS

Remember the parable Jesus told,
  About the Good Samaritan that helped a poor soul.
    He was robbed and beaten, and left for dead,
      it wasn't the priest or the Levi, NO,
    but a Samaritan man that helped him instead.

This is one story we should hold dear, it's about helping others throughout the year. No matter what color, shape, or size, we are all God's children in His eyes.

How you treat, others will return to you. The Bible tells us to **"Do unto others as you would have them do unto you."** Another simple message that yet remains true: **"When you bless others, God blesses you."** Therefore, who have you helped today, or did you just pass by too? Do not do as the priest and the Levi do or else it will come back on you.

Take heed to the Word of God and try to understand. God has a heart for His people that is why Jesus came in the form of a Man, to demonstrate God's love toward you and me. Jesus helped redeem man and took back the keys. He broke the bondage and set the captives free.

Now, helping others, helps you is an example we are to follow through, we are to show love to our fellow man. It is the second in command: ***"Love your neighbor as yourself."***

Trust and believe it will be on a test. Our Greatest Help is made of Heaven's best. He came; He died, and rose again, He gave Creation a second chance. So, remember these words and stand in fear, that if you do not help others; He will not help you!

MILLION DOLLAR PRIZE

He stepped up to me with his shiny smile, I was ready to go with him like "Girls gone wild." He had me hooked and I didn't want to let go.

He had me doing things I never thought I'd do. He got me caught up in this world of glitz, glamour, money, and fame. But when looking at my true self, I brought shame to my name.

When looking at all the material things he gave. It wasn't as valuable to what I gave and for that price, I could have had an unknown disease that could've ended my life.

He came with more things, pleading for me to stay. But I woke up wondering why I stayed with an ice pack to my face. I must have been crazy in thinking that he can change. I was blinded by the expensive worldly things he'd always bring. I thought if I stay one more day I would soon see a wedding ring. Well…who am I fooling, the only rings that I've seen is the one that stings.

Finally, I prayed, "Lord help me this day; I don't want to continue living this way. It's not worth the price of my life, but in you there must be a better way. I thought he was my melting pot, but his actions changed my point of view."

I am a lovely creation that is treasured by you. I deserve to be treated like royalty instead of living in sin and making my bed in Hell." As my eyes were opened to see that I am far more valuable than any earthly things.

A million-dollar prize lives inside of me, I am a precious gem designed from glory. They treat me like I matter to them, when I call upon his name. There's no greater love than giving up his home in Heaven to save a wretch like me. He did it so all might come and be redeemed.

OUT THE BACK DOOR

As I head out the back door, I was stopped in my tracks. Did you pray before opening that door? No, I didn't, but let me explain: I'm running behind schedule and have no time for delay. I have a million of things to do today that are on my agenda, But I'm sorry that wasn't on my to-do list today.

It must have slipped my mind, let me pencil that in later today. I thought I was forgetting something, oh well I will do it another day and anyway I got to go.

It is now day 2, as I head toward the back door, I stop and ponder, thinking to myself, "Did I forget something again? Oh well got to go!" By day 4, my body is slowing down and my energy is low; am I sick? I don't feel sick, well whatever it is it has to go.

As my head rest upon my pillow, a voice came to me: "With all your hurrying you still forgot about me." I answered, "Who are you?" The voice replied, "How can you ask me this after all I've done for you?"

I've made sure traffic was clear for you to keep you safe. The dark blue truck that was speeding down the street, I made him stop at the red light before you drove off yesterday. The young lady that was pushing the stroller with her baby, the baby threw the rattle on the ground before she crossed the street.

I said all this to say, I have protected you each day and made your pathway clear. But you didn't even say "Thank You, not even a simple prayer."

Sitting there as my heart dropped to the floor, "Lord, I'm sorry I left you on that day. Thank you for keeping me and the mercy you gave. Thank You for the overall protection throughout each day. You are more than worthy by saying; Lord go before me this day and guide me in your perfect peace! Amen!"

I'VE FALLEN, AND I CAN'T GET UP

When I think about the many times I fell and sometimes it was face first. But I am glad that I was able to get back up. The Lord has blessed me with his presence. When I wanted to cry and the many trials I faced were just too heavy for me.

Every time I tried to walk away, your love draws me back to you. But how can I be with you when I am clothed in disgrace, guilt, and shame. The urge of wanting to run away has been put at ease, not knowing what to do, I cried: "Lord, I hit rock bottom and I don't know what's left for me to do. I thought that planning my escape was all I could do."

But Lord I am grateful to you for showing me a better way, it is in your light my path has become clear to see. You have always been there, but I was blind and couldn't see. I am reminded that if I fall and can't get up, I am to pray without ceasing.

"Father, forgive me for I slipped today. I let anger, bitterness, and frustration get the best of me (today); especially when I should have given it all to you and just walk away. But instead I got in the way, now it's worse than before. Father, I need you to help me through and let your glorious presence lead me."

Abba Father, please take control I don't want to lead without you. Forgive me if I cause someone else to fall, I don't want to guide no one in the wrong path.

Thank you for keeping me still, even during my storms. Wash me, O Lord from the impurities of the world and make me white as snow. Following you is the best thing I can ever do, you make me better so I don't ever want to get loose. Heavenly Father, I need you 24/7.

Thank You Father! Amen!

WHEN WORDS CUT DEEP

Too many words they cut so deep when you speak, As if it was a bullet from a gun, blood was splash. Too many emotional wounds, yet the same scar is reopened again. Only to ignite a fight and later we forget why.

Where is the love that we once knew?
Where is the love that brought me to you?
How can we get back to what we used to have?
How can we fall back in love again?

Too many memories of a broken heart, no bandage is strong enough to mend the pieces that are scattered apart. Too many disappointments to name, while still they try to discredit you with shame. Now no longer excepting ill fate, I am putting it in the backseat. All those past mistakes, no longer allowing words to cut right through me. But getting that protective covering from one who is the greatest in all things. The One who knew me.

So, goodbye to pain, shame, and misery, you've been evicted from my residency. No longer will I let you hold me down nor allow my space to be invaded by such calamity. I'm breathing better and moving forward, finally free at last. You can keep your indignant words that once cut me deep, but my wounds are healed by the Lord's love and sovereignty. His words to me soothe my soul and embrace me while encouraging me not to let go because I am His!

Kelamenter M. Smith

IN SECRET

The door slightly opens as he peeks inside pretending to be sleep, but inside I wanted to cry. Why does the pain still linger on when you're young of age, but still know what's going on daring to have an innocent face.

Too strong to fight and too weak to stand, life flashed before my eyes he was in control and I followed his command. It made no difference to him, he was determined to state his claim, his pleasure my pain.

What was taught to us about the birds and the bees wasn't nothing compared to the pain I had. Why would he say he love me, but hurt me just the same? I could never be convinced that, both love and pain were the same.

He came with gifts like Santa on Christmas day, thinking that these trinkets will erase the memory. The look, the touch as he came near me, I shrill the moment he was in arms' reach. No one really understood why, they thought I was being difficult, but deep down inside I want to die.

This wasn't the type of love I heard about in God. Why did He let so many things happen that passed everyone's eyes? Was I not good enough to be protected by them?

What did I do to cause this grief? Too many skeletons yet remain, but to me they are all the same. Too many doors that stayed open for the enemy to step in, not enough knowledge to close all of them.

Eliminating the past to move into a brighter future and watch God restore what was battered and broken once more. So precious Lord take my hand, help me to break the enemies' band. This grip is so tight, but I'll take my chances with you. Just to be released and free in You, I can't ask for a better way to live again!

DON'T THROW IN THE TOWEL

"Today was the worst day ever" is what we are used to saying when our day does not go well, you wished you could restart the day. Well what if you could restart a week, a month, or even a year. This is exactly how I feel, if I could push the pause button and push rewind, I would.

But Lord, since that cannot happen I come to you. I am laying all my cares at your feet. It was such a heavy load, I do not want to pick it back up. It seemed as if my whole world was caving in, as if the end of my rope has reached its maximum knots.

I cried and prayed, then prayed and cried. It felt as if you did not hear me, but I know you did. I know this to be true, you sent angels my way to comfort, strengthen, and hold me in my weakest moments.

They whisper through prayer, "Don't Give Up, Don't Give In, and You Can Make It." As I drifted off to sleep, there it was your love and peace overshadowed and gave me rest for my weary soul!

DO YOU SEE WHAT I SEE?

Here I sit and stare wondering, why I cannot see You there, the me, God wants me to be I still can't see. When I turn to the left, I see the me others want me to be but that's not what I was called to be. Yet still having trouble focusing on the real me. Who am I, is what I really want to know. Trying to find my own way without the correct pavement to follow.

When I turn to the right, I see the me that the enemy wants me to be, but Heaven forbid, if I choose that path. The road of destruction as the enemy sits back and laughs.

Lord, I tried to do it my way, but now it is just a huge mess. I cannot help, but to ask for assistance through this stress. My eyes are too cloudy to look forward, but I can only pray that my guardian angels will guide me through. Remove the blockage from my eyes so that I can see, the me, you created me to be.

Then I can answer your question, "Do you see what I see?" My answer will be the child of God for which you created me to be. I am your marvelous work, I am your child, and fearfully and wonderfully made. Thank you Lord for your love is so amazing!

THE GREAT ESCAPE

It was a day like no other, a day I wish had never come. If it was a dream I would've gone back to sleep just to have a different one. I tried everything I could to get through this day in peace, but my flesh kept rising like it was my mouthpiece. No, no, no I am not going there today, no good will come of it. So, I'm going to close my eyes just to see if I'm still asleep.

Ouch! I had to pinch myself too. Now this is way too much for little old me. I'm pondering why this day of all days, why this one had to come. Why couldn't I have had a day like yesterday that was more fun? The taste of bitter sweet fills this day, the fight for life, and the enemy on my trail. Throwing everything my way, but I refuse to give in, today is not the day.

I had to cry out, "Oh Lord help me, save me, and guide me in this day. The enemy is hounding me and I don't know how much more I can take. You are the only one I know that can help me, therefore I'm trusting in you. There is no one else I rather call on, but you."

So please put my mind at ease when I think of you. Your words help direct me and replenish me too. I will not lose heart and dare not give way. The Father always gives you strength when you pray and the great escape!

AND ALL THINGS WERE MADE NEW

I kept telling myself, "Trust the process, and that it's going to be better." Taking my eyes off the situation and looking to the Father was hard enough, but I did it.

I don't recall putting on bitterness, resentment, and envy, but I wore them daily like new clothes. Feeling like what the use, it's not worth the hassle no more, I'm done. But the Holy Spirit told me, "Don't give up."

I was trying hard not to fight it, but I cried even more. Lord, please open at least one door, it would give me hope and courage to move on. Yet still working despite my situation trying not to fret or worry. But when doubt seems to creep in, all I could do was cry out even louder and harder.

Gasping for air and wet with tears. Father, if you hear me please give me strength and courage to make it through. I am holding on to my belief that you have the power and authority to change my situation. Because in Christ all things were made new!

Kelamenter M. Smith

NOW I KNOW

It is clear to me that you've changed, All the signs are there right before my eyes. I thought by now life would be different for us, but that was falsified by the here and now. No more can one soul take to live in a place like this, restless nights and worrisome days.

I was fooled into thinking you could provide a new life for me to live in. Blinded by your sweet ambitions and my childlike ways, I thought for sure that this would be the one...but, now I know. Knowing the very thing you thought was good for you turned out to be so wrong, how could I have been so blind?

Listening to your charming words had my life twisting and turning. Close those doors to what was scarce and pure, trying to turn me into the devil's advocate with no cure. Who, but one can hear my cry? Who, but one can save me from that life of torment? Who has power enough to kick the butt out of Hell?

Then why think that I'm too deep in sin that I cannot be saved. What makes my sin different from yours? Confessing them and learn from the past mistakes then keep moving forward. It is very clear to me that the life I was use too is no more. While you pretend to be concern when you care less.

What was the use in salvaging this relationship when all I felt was pain?

Now, my heart feels different because things have changed. The voice that use to make my heart flutter, now has burnt a hole in that place... but, now I know.

All I can say is, "Precious Lord take my hand, lead me from this forsaken land and to a place where I can bloom again!"

DON'T RUN AWAY FROM ME

When you love someone that is when it is hard to let them go. The clinch of a hard-long pinch is the feeling I have in my heart. Contemplating inside about what is really going on, not wanting to face the actuality that being with you wasn't the best thing.

We tried to get through all the debris, but it was nonsense; we knew it was never meant to be. We tried to pretend the love was good, but later questioned:

"Why are we playing these games?"

The love used to be there, but now it is like a show, so no one will see the real deal. This is not a phase or a midlife crisis, the love we had dwindled away. To me it felt more and more like an obligation and not an ounce of dedication to love. The facts remain this love is at a crossroad, burdened with despair trying to find a home and lay its head.

Feeling like a helpless sparrow that cannot fly,

looking up to the sky and saying to myself "why?"

> How many nights have we sat and prayed
> for answers to be true?
>
> How many wasted days, when nothing
> was said to you?
>
> Should I've looked the other way when you
> turned your back on me?
>
> Should I have stayed to work it out hoping
> you don't run away from me?

Behind the thin glass the misery was there, we just didn't let it show. Too many people would be affected by this to just let it go. No love should hurt to where it feels like hell. Treat me the way you want to be treated, like you are on cloud nine living well.

I guarantee I'll have you singing sweet melodies, you'll rush home every time you hear our song with words that can't be explained. Safe in my arms and in harmony, smiling wide, and thinking heaven is where I want to be!

TRUST APPLY POWER
(TAP)

There were more of "one of those days" then I have ever experienced before. I have seen things like what I was in, but never really experienced it. The feeling of neglect ran across my mind a few times but I very quickly cast that thought out. I know firsthand of what my Father can do. But there were days where I was ready to tap out, afterward of feeling out of energy. I sat and meditated on the word TAP. With each difficult day, I would take the word TAP and begin to use it in my prayers.

Father, in you I will Trust, and I will Apply your Holy Word to my situation, for I know that all Power is yours and there is nothing too hard for you. You see my situation and are working things out for my good, even when it doesn't feel good. So, I will continue to do what you have called me to do. Thank you for taking care of all my needs in accordance to your will, so I will hold on until then.

I will T.A.P. into Your Holy Ghost power and keep my faith active when my flesh gets weak. I will, *"Trust in the Lord with all my heart, and lean not on my own understanding; in all my ways acknowledge Him, and He shall direct my paths."* Proverbs 3:5,6 (NKJV). I will *"incline my ear to wisdom, and **Apply** my heart to understanding."* Proverbs 2:2 (NKJV).

I believe *"God is my strength and power, and He makes my way perfect."*

2 Samuel 22:2 (NKJV).

~AMEN~

WHEN LIFES' PRESSURE POINTS ARE PUSHED

Bill Collectors. House Notes. Student loans racing in default. Noisy Neighbors. Car will not cooperate. Jobs flirting with bankruptcies. Bosses look to you for answers and you're feeling confused.

Stock market dances in declining discos. Banks are in harmony with mob-like ways, one bad move and you're destined for doom. Mixed roles, but they both try to wear the pants.

Reality shows are orchestrated based on ratings. Churches have become the mix-n-mingle club (not all churches fit in this category, but is God truly getting all the glory).

Fewer doctors and more patients than they can handle. For the next generation, FAFSA has become the new way to income. Dependents need dependents and less independence is achieved.

Misguided and Abused Education, Illegal practices, fixed games, and things. Crooks, thugs, and gangsters are handling critical businesses. Law-abiding citizens are targeted by authorities' mind games.

Unemployment and the Homeless are beyond the margin, yet no one is trying to decrease it. Countries fight to stay alive within their own kind.

Lord God, if we don't wake-up soon, we will all miss your timing and signs. Standing in the middle of nowhere trying to find somewhere to go, but anywhere is looking pretty darn good.

You try to categorize every situation as your head hurts more; it is not your place to do it so why even try. You must know that when life pressure points are pushed, there is a way to push back without retaliation. This battle is not about you, this battle is all spiritual. Now choose this day who you will serve!

SURRENDER, RETREAT, OR STAND STRONG

When your back is up against the wall and it seems as if nothing is working at all. When your friends and family turn their backs on you, when the weight gets too heavy to hold, what will you do?

When your cries go unanswered and the tear stain remains on your pillow. When your walk gets harder and longer, when the only relief is when your sleep, but awaken back into reality searching for peace, what do you do?

When it seems like Hell's torture has invaded your home and no one hears your aching groans. No matter how hard you yell or cry, no rescue was in sight. You do everything, even plead your case, but even more it felt like a waste of time. You pace back and forth throughout the day waiting expertly for a release to come, what will you do?

Misguided and Abused Education, Illegal practices, fixed games, and things. Crooks, thugs, and gangsters are handling critical businesses. Law-abiding citizens are targeted by authorities' mind games.

When the battlefield leaves a smothering smell of defeat. When the little bit of strength left in your body begin to fade, what do you do? When your heart is broken and wounded by harsh words, bad choices, and people. When your joy seems like a distant memory that you pray would return some day, what do you do?

By now you're at the brink of destruction ready to throw in the towel, but you can't. It is when that soft inner voice says, "Don't Give Up."

Lord God, when you have taken all that you can take, and nothing is breaking. Will you surrender to defeat? Will you revert back and retreat to your old ways? Or will you stand strong in your faith that God will come? What would you do? Keep holding on 'til your change come!

NOW THIS

Just when you thought, the storm was over, a surprise tornado pops out of nowhere destroying everything in its path. You want to scream out "I have had enough" but what good will that do anyway. You've tried everything in your power to get past all the pain, but life brings more disappointments to add to the pain.

When will the residue subside so joy can come in? You want to feel happy again and gain the promised land you dreamed of, but was it just a dream? When will your silver-lining burst through those dark clouds? When will the old songs "Oh Happy Day" will come for you?

Although, right now these days have been not so good, my happy days are not far. Sometimes it's hard to pray when in pain, you just want that feeling to be gone. You just want to smile again. But when bad days become habitual, it seems that you can't comprehend what good days feel like.

The breaking of a generational curse is necessary to get passed those similar traits that seem to pass from generation to generation. No longer feeling the sting of poverty, abuse, fear, and loneliness, those days are long gone and the curse is broken.

Walking in a newness of life and in the light that reestablished me into the holy family. My eyes are open to see the storms for what they were truly meant to be, a stepping stone for others, a refinery.

However, as the days, months, and years go by you wonder how faraway those Hallelujah days are. But the actuality is a little bit of rain often helps the earth flourish for blooming seasons. It is just a matter of how you look at the situation. So, despite my hard days and there have been plenty, I will see myself as a Kadupul flower, a rare beauty and nothing less!

FAILURE IS NOT AN OPTION

Today, we see many things and people take the option of "throwing in the towel" when the going gets tough. The world has created a barrier causing us to feel that if we are not making enough, we are considered poor and in poverty. The various labels the world tries to wrap us in is harsh and cruel.

Bound by opposition of sin not allowing forgiveness to settle in, your back in the same wilderness again, only to find that it's much harder this time around. Two steps forward, five steps back, can't help, but to look at what's not happening and do an evaluation of myself.

To do a self-evaluation is not to say that you're unhappy with yourself, but shifting into a different direction. My aspect is failure is not an option, so long as I'm in Christ. It is through him and by him I can have a divine expected end, an expected end with no regrets!

NOTHING ELSE MATTERS

I wonder, have you ever found yourself at a crossroad?

Pondering what you should do, but still stuck at the crossroads. The opportunity to look at all angles to weigh the cost. The thought of being correct was lost. Never in my wildest dreams would I have thought of this happening, but it did.

They say experience is a good teacher, well I plan to ace this test. I refuse to let this get the best of me and deny the worse of me. My future is far too valuable for me to lose.

Serving you with great expectation, and giving you glory will bring joy and gladness to the lives we touch. Therefore, when it comes to you, I'm all in and I'm made full in your presence. Nothing else matter, when I'm with you because you make my world right and in unison in you!

TOUGH AS NAILS

Repeatedly I told myself this too shall pass. I'm coming out on top when my faith is in the true King. I'm reminded of the old saying: "What doesn't kill me will make me stronger." Well I must be tough as nails cause the situation

I'm in from the physical eyes, I can't win. Nevertheless, since I know better, I am more than a conqueror through Him that loves me. My Jehovah Jireh is always on time, even when I'm down to my last. So, a little faith is all it takes and watch, what prayer can do.

I started small, but bigger testimonies evolved and now I'm working even harder for the kingdom, singing "How Great Thou Are." Take it from me because I've been there not knowing which way to go. However, I had to learn to take my hands, mouth and eyes off it and send it all to Heaven. My Father can handle it better than I can!

DEEPLY WOUNDED, BUT I'M NOT BROKEN

The disappointment, the hurt, and shame that I am faced with, is more than I can bear. Crying through the late nights hours asking myself "How did I get here and how do I get out of here?"

Somebody prayed for me because my sanity had no peace and my soul no sleep. No rest for the weary, yet looking toward Heaven for the answers to meet my life's needs. Every wrong move made it harder and harder to get closer to the one that set the captives free.

Wounded and downtrodden, but I'm not broken. Barely standing firm in what little faith I have left. Wanting with everything within me to kick, fuss, and scream, But that won't change anything, therefore I prayed.

Father, forgive me for not trusting your word. I do believe you have everything under control and you know what is best for me. So, as I look to you to ease my concerns and doubts. Please grant me more peace in my heart and in my home, cleanse both places because there, is where I want you to roam. concerns and doubts. Please grant me more peace in my heart and in my home, cleanse both places because there, is where I want you to roam.

So, precious Lord takes my hands and guides me through. I am grateful for everything you do. Please fill this emptiness inside and comfort me each day. Father, I pray that your will be done. Despite the hardship, I know you are the True Almighty one. Please grant me a peaceful sleep and a hedge of protection to rest easy. Amen!

SEE IT BEFORE IT HAPPENS

Unspoken words that whisper in one's mind, you can have what you say, so believe you will receive it and it shall happen. Dreams of a better life, better career, better family, and a better me is what I want to see. But reality hit me hard, I'm left with traces of hopes and lots of despair.

A prisoner in the world has more freedom than a prisoner in ones' mind. You have limited space to dream, to hope, and to create. Your confined by the past and it warps the very thought pattern you manage to save, finding strength to stand. Clear away all the pollution and delusion of what your life will be by the tainted scope of the past. Instead of peeping into the future and perceiving a phenomenal life that the Supreme Being designed for you and me.

Finally getting closer to my ultimate Creator and grasping an unprecedented view of being adopted by you. My life has never been the same and my view has changed. I see clearly now that I am following you. You have made me complete and allow me to see my future before it happens!

Our homeland is crying and souls quickly dying, no political leader can help you. The call is up to you, cry out to the Lord and he'll answer your call. He has been waiting to hear your voice and enter your heart. In all the chaos and pain, no one to turn too, just call on the King of Kings because Heaven knows!

HEAVEN KNOWS

Our homeland is crying, but they say they don't know why. How can you smile, and then lie? Too many years wasted away, too many souls that gave in to the enemy. While some play church thinking it's okay; fame and fortune will not save you come Judgment Day.

Our homeland is dying, but they don't have a clue, or do they? While we are played like fools, one lie, two lies, three lies more, another high-top leader headed toward destruction's door.

One by one we all fall, but do they know about the aftermath behind the sting. We look at the reports and say, "Lord, where are you?" But where were we, where were the parents to say the least. We act as if the Creator of this world has blinders on, like he doesn't see. Is it that we, ourselves have been blind all along?

The Father is listening, he sees, and he knows, but how many times have we closed the door to his opened arms. He waited and waited, but it is now time for urgency. Know that time waits for no one, get your life right before it's too late.

I'M IN TOO DEEP

Soul-searching, why do we call it that when we are self-searching?

What made me advance in the direction that drives me to stay?

With all the troubles in this life, I felt compelled to cave in.

But I'm not a quitter, nor do I want the enemy to win or at least think he did.

Besides learning from the Bible the way that I did, I'm in too deep to turn away.

So, I might as well stay in this course and finish the race.

My team is already set and my tools are already in place,

Now I must stand in position as the Most High sets the pace!

CRY NO MORE

This season seems a little harder than before, as if a locomotive came in full throttle. The pain still subsides as I try to remove its stain that was left on my heart.

Whoever said love hurts must have been down that road because I'm on that road too. Thinking that things would get better but the illusion in my mind did not go according to time. Now abandoned by the false vision, I was so eager to find, but it vanished with the feelings I had.

If love is a two-way street, then what happened to me? I must have missed a turn because I am at a dead–end. Locked away the empty hole to my heart, it can never be filled again. Wishing that this was all a bad dream, but the reality is, it's in living color.

No how-to books can help me, no motivation, or song to help bring me through. I need something stronger to breakthrough. Why does it have to hurt this bad, especially from you even when you've done all you can.

No appreciation for the time that was wasted. Just a broken heart and painful tears that want you to remain. But when the refreshing comes to you can feel whole again. So, get up out of that dreary place and wipe your face. You are beautiful to me, no more looking at what others can do, but look at what I can do for you.

I allowed all this to make you strong and open your eyes to see that nothing in this world can hold its own unless I allow it to be. Being true to me in your weakest hours is what I want from you. To seek me first for all things and to remove the wall from your heart.

I come not to hurt you nor cause you despair, but to build you up and to let you know I do care. So, you don't have to cry no more, I am here for you, my dear!

BROKEN PIECES

Shattered pictures, broken dreams. You came to me incorrectly telling me "I'm not the best", while trying to make a scene. In one embarrassing moment, I ran and hid, torn and confused by the humiliation. You tried to come back into my life thinking everything was okay now. But today you will feel what it's like to lose face.

No longer trusting you as a friend, I consider you to be my nemesis. You mangled my character various times I thought you were a true pal in which I could confide, however, all your true colors came through. The fake ones were just a mirage. You deceived me far too long with your dirty camouflage. But right now, you will not take up space to hurt me again, You are dismissed ex-friend.

Putting the pieces back together again I'm more conscious of who I call friend A true friend will stand by you through thick and thin. They're not out for selfish gain, but value the bond that is shared between the two of you. They are willing to give credit when credit is due.

A true friend will not expose your weakness and secret pain, but honor your life as you do the same. Be fair, be true, and always remember this "A true friend despite your faults will love you for you!"

HEALED AND REDEEMED

The day is glistening with bright beams from the sky. As the room's door opens widely the doctor and his trainees' walks in with an unsettling look upon their faces. "I am amazed and dumbfounded regarding your test results. I mean I have a good report to give you. We checked and checked but nothing was found."

As I smiled at the doctors and thought, "Well doc, you just don't know who is my true healer." But as the doctor continues to explain, I smiled and listened. "The results are here and everything is clear, you don't have to have the surgery. You will be going home tomorrow."

As I smiled, one of the trainees looked my way and said, "It was a blessing to assist you!" I said, "Thank You!" The next morning, I awoke with such a joy in my spirit. I was healed before surgery took place and my Savior redeemed me by His amazing grace!

LOOK AGAIN

Lord, when I look back at my situation and all the hell I've gone through. Nothing around me was working for my good. All I did was sit, thinking that I was at the end of my rope and couldn't tie no more. But I was told to look again and when I obey, the Father said it could have been much worse without Him.

The Lord says, "I will turn everything that has become stumbling blocks into stepping stones for your good. For those that don't believe will be in awe of what I will bring you too. Don't be sadden by the exterior of your life, just know that I am rearranging and organizing some things for you, just trust me."

In a vulnerable state, all I could say was "Thank you Lord." I was glad that I am loved enough to be informed of the shifting that is coming into place in my life. Therefore, I encourage you not to give up, if your hope is in things above and not in things on Earth.

If your season is unpleasant, say "this too shall pass." If you're in a dry place and no light has beamed its rays your way, just say "this too shall pass." When your world is turned upside down and nowhere to run you can say to yourself, "this too shall pass." Keep waiting while the process circulates into the divine plan and watch how better your life will be!

THE WAKEUP CALL

It's 4 a.m. when the call came in.
    I looked at my phone dreading to hear,
    But to be sure I had to take the call.
    While preparing myself my voice cracked saying:

    Hello, this is she
No, it's ok, I see...uh huh.... well how can that be
(sigh in disbelief) what does that have to do with me?
I've been there since ninety-six and now you're telling me
to hit the bricks. I don't understand, why me.... And it's
my fault this happened...no, no I get it.... Why tell me this
when I already do... yeah, yeah same to you (click).

Does this sound familiar or is the conversation
    quite the same?
It may take only one phone call to make your whole life change or even one bad event that have you rethinking, revamping, and renewing your life again.

There are times when we are faced with an epiphany. There is your chance to interchange into a new lane. You have been given another chance and try not to mess this up again!

DESPERATELY SEEKING JESUS

Lord, I come searching high and low. Seeking you for answers to what I don't know. Barring the pain of not knowing where you are. I'm trying to find a way to get to where you are.

Lord, I desperately need you to show me where to go. I'm longing for your touch to help ease my pain once more. What must I do for you to call my name? Listening to the winds and I don't hear a thing. And seeking shelter from the stormy rain.

I'm crying and calling out to you O Lord. Where are you Lord, I really need you? As I close my eyes and to my surprise, I began to feel your presence inside.

You said you've been there the whole time even when I couldn't find you. It's not that you weren't there, except I couldn't see. Now I understand why we need a strong relationship with the Almighty.

Doubt had stepped in and belittled my faith. I thought I was going to lose my mind but your touch gave me amazing grace. Searching all over to fill those empty places , I know now that your love is the only filler needed to make me whole.

Kelamenter M. Smith

I tried everything else but nothing satisfies like you. You went beyond the surface and touched the roots. No longer am I coming up empty because I know where you are. I hasten my steps to meet with you there and feeling the loving relationship, we share.

So no longer desperate because my soul is satisfied with you. The very soft whisper from you gets me more motivated to do all I can for you (because of you). Thank you Lord for not passing me by, turning my sadness to singing and pains to joy. It's all due to You, I can live again!

ICE - BREAKER

The room is tense but no one moves. No one is backing away from this stand down. The heaviness and sharp looks that would cut you down in a split second when turned toward you.

The raw emotions thicken the air, which made it too hard to breathe. The coughing and sniffling produce by the constant flow of teardrops and anger. Lord, the burning words have been released and we cannot take them back. No one dare say another word or it just might create a bigger explosion.

Lord, if we can use anything right now, we can use an icebreaker to help calm the room. As more tears begin to flow, we both wanted to walk out the door, but no one could; looking at each other thinking,

"What were we arguing for anyway?"

Our faces, emotions, and reactions has changed from bitterness and anger to remorse and compassion. Lord, we need you to guide us in our natural actions to react in a defensive state when our triggers are activated. Then we are reminded of your word, "Everyone must be quick to hear, slow to speak, and slow to anger." James 1:19 (NIV). Although the damage was done, but saying "I'm sorry" just won't do.

You go one way, I'll go the other way, and pray. Sometimes you wonder "what's the use, they will never understand no matter how hard you try to explain it to them." They say time heals all wounds, but:

>What about a reopened scar?
>Does that need extra time to heal?
>What about the broken pieces?
>What about the broken-hearted?

Yes, time will heal all wounds when Christ is the mender and your soul salvation. All he asks is that you come ~ all are welcome to enter!

THIS TIME I'LL WIN

Beaten down by the weight of the world, wondering what is going on. You hustle and bustle for daily living, but still left out in the cold. How could this be?

I've done everything required of me and yet I'm standing alone. Why has this happened and where can I go to call my home?

> No love was shown, no bread in which to be fed.
> Feeling so desolate, but it was all in my head.
> No one really understands me but the Almighty.
> Why am I feeling this way, does anyone care for me?
> The enemies hold on me has me feeling destitute.

> Broken in spirit is all I see, blinded by the mere fact
> that there is one who truly loves me.
> But afraid as to what He might see behind the décor,
> is my impurity.

Release me from your devious ways, You wicked entity. I don't belong to you anyway. I am a servant to the Heavenly King. No more of my space will give way to you, for my Savior is Jesus Christ my Lord. You taunted me far too long but by the grace of God I've been restored. No longer defeated by the enemies' plots and plans, by Jesus Christ this time I'll win!

Kelamenter M. Smith

SEASONS OF LIFE

As the fall season is laid to rest and the new season rolls in, the world changes its colors among most things. From bright red to burnt orange, one by one they all change before falling to the ground. It is amazing how trees and other things let us know when the seasons are shifting.

The flowerbeds go from full to almost bare. The "V" signs in the sky the birds form when winter comes. The farmers harvest their crops to give the land rest until next season.

Unlike these signs, the changes in ones' life are not so obvious to the physical eyes. Sometimes it is after the season has shifted that you can see the transformation.

The various seasons in your life enter in like mood swings. Sometimes the seasons come in like a raging storm or sometimes it comes in like a whistling wind. However it comes to you this year, do not let it overthrow you to the point of depression, there is hope in the midst of it all.

Find that quiet garden to release your sadness and regain your joy. Wipe your tears away and see the glory of the Lord in that place. When resting in the Almighty hand that brings barren things to life, walk into the garden of bountiful and watch the Master at work!

GET UP AND GET MOVIN'

$\mathcal{D}$epression is a state of mind, a feeling of loneliness, destitution, and emptiness. It takes the whole body down with it. It covers you like a big old blanket and after a while it becomes comfortable. It was easy to slip into that desolate place, where no light, no hope, and no love satisfies that area.

It's dry, dull, and lifeless, the colors are dark and gray. Yet something in me keeps telling me I can make it, but how can I get beyond this dreary state? You keep telling me that there is hope, but where was it when I needed it the most? This can't be the end I kept telling myself, there must be something better than this. As I began crying out to the Lord, it was the beginning, the breaking of the cycle.

With each passing day, I took back a piece of me, with each passing day, I gain more and more strength. But I couldn't do it on my own, I need Jesus to bring me to the top. I felt replenished and it never felt so good, rebirth with a new vision and renewed dreams. And never look back at the has-been, look toward the what-will-be through Christ. He wants all or nothing!

AGAINST ALL ODDS

When life seems to have you by the brow, shake loose and set yourself free. When the weight of this world is upon your shoulders, stand on the Word that is powerful and true.

Even when your back is against the wall and it seems like there is no help for you. Remember that God's power is against all odds. In Him you can win.

When life seems to have you pinned down with more issues then you can take, remember that the Father will never put more on you than you can bear. Pray for strength to endure and assurance during the tests and trials.

Understanding that it was given to you, it was not without purpose. Even when you feel like you're at your breaking point and you're ready to explode.

Go to the altar and release it all right there. No one said you have to stay in defeat, but you can overcome when your trust is in the Lord of Lords!

MISSION ACCOMPLISHED

The day I met you was oh so real, Everyone praised You upon entering Jerusalem. The sound rings my ears with joy as the people shouted "Hosanna to the Son of David!" "Blessed is he who come in the name of the Lord!" "Hosanna in the highest!"

As the wave of happiness blankets the crowd. They still did not know your true purpose and plan. They thought being in the in-crowd was a high demand. They assumed that the King of all, was coming to possess the land and make his claim. They were wrong.

The day I met you was oh so real, to the untrained eyes, you look like a commoner, but there was nothing common about you. It took the purging of the temple for us to see that You are serious about the Father's business. The whole world was in an uproar about this man that imprinted the cities and towns. Some asked "Who is this man?"

But never seek God in regard to Him, they just assumed him to be another prophet, crazy, and deranged. Little did they know or showed little concern of your presence and authority to remove, redeem, and redirect man back to the Father.

LIVING BEYOND SELF: Searching For Meaning

You stayed straight on the course and the order was blueprinted in some of their hearts. New revelations of the prophecy being fulfilled by You, Now they know and not many believed.

The day I met You was oh so real. You called my name. My heart pounded, and began to swelter at the very thought of You. I froze, looking around my eyes only saw the tangible things. You called my name again, my throat was lodged with fear in answering. My heart said "Yes" but nothing was vocal. Therefore I hid, wanting to scream for help, but who would understand.

Just like back then, you came prepared with your plan. You impress yourself in my mind and I can't stop thinking about You. You caught my attention and my pursuit of You still continues from my adolescent years. I will not stop, I want to hear you say: "Well done, my good and faithful servant!"

RECOVERY

We know that all wounds take time to recover, but the scar is still visible. It has been reinjured repeatedly, praying for healing, to conceal the sore within. What about the things that were taken from you without just cause? On the inside, you want to fight, fuss and say some unholy words, but you realize that the stuff can be replaced.

In a world where we daily see turmoil running rampant; how can we remain faithful when those hurtful stages that cause us pain and frustration hangs around still? What about the time that was stolen from us? Do we try to do everything that we miss, or do we just let time slip away?

How will I know if what I was called to do is really my true destiny or what I deeply desire to do is contrary to what you want me to do? Will you not help me oh Lord, I am lost without your guidance. Nonetheless, I still feel like I'm in a line for recovery, but I can't do it completely without you. Heavenly Father, please help me!

THIS FIGHT IS NOT MINE

The battle we face are oftentimes long and hard, but it puts our faith in perspective. We either going to walk in it or fall out of it.

> Who can say their life is their own?
>
> Who dare to say they made their own wealth?
>
> Who would say they were the ones that did it all?
>
> How bold are we to say we don't need anybody when the fact remains that we are all connected in some way?

The battles we face are often used to either get us in gear moving forward or more so to see what we're made of. We must remember who are our true Maker is and our purpose in life. Boasting and prideful thinking brings failure at some point in one's life. We are to show humility and love, for blessings can bring out the true us. The flesh gets weak, but in Christ we are made strong, don't let the flesh control you.

The battles we face are not that of our peers, families, or others, but the battle is within. It's not about us, it's all about the Master of the universe. So remember that this fight is not mine or yours it's the Lord of Lord's, will fight your battles just give it to Him, for in Him there is victory!

TELL THE STORY

To tell the story of how it used to be, you wouldn't believe it anyway. You had to be there. To tell the story of how it should have been, you would only think of it in past tense, you just had to be there to understand.

Listen to my story and unfold the truth of all the hurt, lies, and tears that were cried. You say "no," I say "yes," let me tell the story of what you don't know. The agony and defeat of being me. It was a love-n-hate type of feeling. The person I wanted to be, wasn't what was before me or that's what I felt to be true.

To tell the story from the outside trying to look in, is just a mere fabrication or a preview of my story. To tell such a story must come from the main source or even the Master Creator if you want the truth.

No one can tell your story like you nor can anyone live in your shoes and tell the same story. We all have our own version of our story, others' story, and our story of our start to salvation.

The main story is you are saved and live to share your story leading to Christ!

THE STRUGGLES WITHIN

Hiding behind the closed doors. Wondering over past mistakes and now questioning if the call is real or fake. Pounding in my head, you're not the one. So why not hide or run, but the nagging in my heart tells me I'm on the right path, trust your instinct and always pray.

After the repeat sessions of real or fake, stay, or run, I am so confused. Lord I want to do whatever it is you have called me to do. I've been living a double life far too long, I just want a place to belong. A peaceful place that I can call home and have rest for my mind, body, and soul.

I used to think I was too worthless to be used by you, But now I know that you do have a special need of me. The fight within against the hand of time I must decide fast.

If I don't follow you, I'm doomed for destruction, but if I follow you I am born anew. There was no doubt at a very young age. I gave my life to Christ and my life has never been the same. Yet working through the changes and eliminating the struggles within!

Perseverance

YET HOLDING ON

Tears after tears when all I could do is pray. Nonetheless, even trying to find the strength to pray is challenging every day, but I do it anyway. It felt as if the whole world and its trouble live in my place. It was like nothing working for me, nor did an open door come my way.

My hope was beginning to fade, but my faith is what kept me through those very hard days. Those days where the storms seem to linger the most. All I wanted was a glimpse of sunlight to break the dark clouds away.

Looking up toward heaven I pray, "Lord please give me strength to endure. Lord there is no other help we know. Please don't withdraw thyself from thee, we have nowhere else to go." Daily the Lord provides for us and brings peace to ease our trouble minds. We have a better understanding of what we confess, "Lord I will trust you, give us this day our daily bread."

So through this season, we are yet holding on, not because of outsiders, but Lord it's all because of you. We would not have made it this far without you. So we thank you for keeping us this long; not allowing us to give up because you have greater plans in store for us.

While we are holding on, we will continue to pray unto the Lord awaiting the day that, even your promises to us are fulfilled. After we believe there is no one like you, which is why we continue to do the work we do for you ~ we Love You!

THE PROBLEM WITH ME
(INSIDE A TROUBLED MIND)

The problem with me is at first, I didn't know how to love me because of the many issues that were carried inside. I smiled on the outside, but in the inside, I cried, and I cried. All I wanted was somebody to love me for me. To show me some affection and not the pain I used to see.

So many days I wonder, "Why God, why me?" but no answer came speedily. My tears soaked my pillow each night as I was the last one to drift off to sleep. Wondering, did I do something wrong for the pain to have come into my home. I prayed many days, Lord if you love me, please take this pain away. I can't keep pretending that everything is ok. When in my reality, I wanted to run away and hide or waste away and die. No, I wasn't contemplating suicide, but the enemy tried to put it in my mind, but I said "NO."

The problem with me is there was a lot of bad stuff in my life that clouded my eyes to see all the good. There was love, but how could I be sure if it is real, I have seen so much pain, it caused me to doubt everything.

> I ask: "God, are you real? If you are, please
> help my family.

Kelamenter M. Smith

I don't know what to do, but ask you. See God, I didn't know how to pray, but my grandmother helped me along the way. She said, if you talk to God with a truthful heart, trust and believe that your prayers would be heard, then your answers will come momentarily."

The problem with me is not me but the enemy that is against me, fighting daily to stay in the race. The enemy showed no remorse or grace, stronger they came too many to name. But an angel of the Lord prayed for me and my strength I regain. Heavenly Father, please renew me and strengthen me where I am weak. Please protect me and my family as we go to sleep. Please guide my family and help us make it through. I don't want to live this life without you!

WHAT MATTERS MOST

When you really think about life, what does it mean to you?

Is it gaining material items that can be thrown away?

Or is it achieving stardom, but in an instant, lose everything?

Isn't life more valuable than material things, stardom, and fame?

What have you done that makes the angels ring the Heavens with your name?

Are you a God pleaser or a man pleaser?

Who are you, with those big brown eyes staring back at me?

I am the one that wants the most out of life the way God intended it to be and not the destruction of humanity.

What matters to me is the things that God cares for the most. Saving as many souls before the era of this life closes. Here today and gone tomorrow is all I have seen. Please don't let one more day go by and not accept the one true King.

Life is too precious to live grudgingly.

Learn to love in all that you say and do.

Be a blessing to others as Jesus was to me and to you!

WHY

Why Lord, why is the pain so hard to bear? If I stay here too long I won't be able to hold up my head. I'm seeking you Oh Lord because there is no one else that can do the things you do. I'm in need of answers or instructions as what to do.

Sometimes I want to scream and cry, when my time will come. When will my big ship roll in? It seems like I've been waiting for so long I just want a piece of Heaven in my home.

Lord, forgive me if I seem frustrated and confused.
I can't do anything except wait on you.

I want to hear your soothing voice that washes away my tears. Oh Lord, your spirit is the only one that brings me comfort and eliminates my fears.

I need you: please to take this hurt from me. I've been crying all night putting myself to sleep. I don't want to try anything else, but you. I believe something so simple you can make anew,

You are my one true friend.

When I was knee deep in mess, you cleared the way and refreshed me once again. A thought enters: "I don't deserve it." I just want my life to end, I rebuke that thought again and again. To soothe my anxiety the Holy Spirit came,

I'm feeling rested in a place that I cannot explain.

I'm sleeping in tranquility like never before.

Trusting in the one that heals and seals all wounded doors!

WHAT KIND OF LEGACY WILL YOU LEAVE?

The news gives us so many bad reports, you hear of killings here and there, child molesters, rapists, terrorists, and not to mention the economy downturn. If you are like me, you are wondering when your ship will come in. Why does it seem like the enemy always wins, but in the end, I will overcome.

The values that were learned, take those to heart and let Jesus in. He is the only one that can help you through this madness. He may be your only friend.

So, what will they say about you when your time has ended?

Will they say that you were a true Christian that did what Jesus did?

Or will they say your walk and talk was just a front to make yourself look good, only to find out that you weren't living like you should?

Kelamenter M. Smith

What kind of legacy will you leave?

Will there be something valuable for your family
to sustain them?

Will your children's children be able to
obtain their claim?

As I treasure every moment as if it was my last, I am making life worth living and leaving a smile at every turn.

    Being true to myself and following God, doing what is right and pursuing a Holy life. I am not all what I should be, but I am glad I am not what I used to be. In pursuit of a Godly life, trying to make the best within this unchurched race. To fulfill my purpose, which was designed for me. Leaving the past behind and looking ahead to where I want to be!

ANOTHER DAY'S JOURNEY

Life is too short to let it pass you by. If the Lord blesses you with one more day, you have a full twenty-four hours to get it right.

Why waste your day with frivolous living?

Some may say another day another dollar, but I say another day another soul to be saved. As each day is granted, I thank the Lord for it. If by chance I don't get it right, I pray Lord please have mercy on me and forgive me for not doing the assignment as I was told to. It's a long walk home but I want as many that will join me to meet with you. So Lord I'm sorry that the happenstance of the souls that I missed saving but please grant me grace and favor for one more day.

Life is too short to let one more day slip away without telling someone about your saving grace. So listen up and listen well. The Savior came mighty and strong in making sure we know where we belong. Just one more step, one more day.

Don't let the enemy have you misconstrued, while dragging you to Hell. Know that there is a better place but the enemy won't tell. Therefore, seek the Lord while he may be found and call upon His name. The Father is waiting for you and the heavens will be rejoicing!

INGENIOUS DECISIONS

Misguided by my sinful pride, I was coerced to join the opposite side.

Seeing all the wrong things I did, I cried.

Please take this cup from me.

I can't handle the agony of the repercussions for the wrong choices. I made it in thinking they were right, but I got played.

Seeing the wicked for who they truly are,
I'm surprised I lived as long as I did.

Making bad decisions one after another,
My life was in shambles as the others.

I am grateful O' Lord that you didn't give up on me.

In understanding the truth, now I see the real deal.

No one else can tell me a tale. I know the difference between Heaven and Hell.

I'm joining you so in repentance my flesh died.

A new me in Christ was born and I'm feeling good.

I'm happy for the right selection that was made.

Living life to the fullness, receiving all that I need.

It is because of you I'm moving forward

And walking in the essence of victory!

Kelamenter M. Smith

I DIDN'T KNOW

As a young adolescent, all you could think about was "when you get older." You talk about the things you will do, the places you will go, and the cars you will drive. However, as you get older your thought pattern changes as your lifestyle changes. Even the people you meet change and your perspective changes.

Now that you're an adult, some are wishing they could go back to the adolescent stage. In those days there was less worry and stress. However, the same excuses lie down within, for many that have stayed in-between eras and don't want to grow or change. The excuse they use is "I didn't know."

For many that have become the most constant excuse to use when it is apparent that you know what is expected of you, but don't do it. But one thing is true, one wrong decision will throw you off course. I didn't know it would make life so much harder, but it did. Paying for your mistakes now will benefit you later.

If you have an "I didn't know" mentality it is best that you work your hardest to understand the value of life. Life is way too short to be playing games!

"Get wisdom, get understanding;"

Proverbs 4:5a (NKJV).

I TRIED

Well, I'm up another night wide awake wondering "Why me?"

Why am I stuck in this misery, praying continuously and still no change?

Lord, I am tired of all this heartache and pain.

When there is no one to talk to, really without an opinionated mind. When, what I really need is to vent for a while, thinking of the wonderful visions you gave me. I'm wondering if they are too far-fetched and can I really obtain them?

So sick and tired of being sick and tired, I cried out: "I don't know what else to do. I have nothing else left in me, fill me Lord with you." I even tried to tie another knot before letting go. I'm just that stubborn to tie three more, but what I do know is that when I've done all I can, keep standing.

Well Lord, I give it all to you because if it's left to me, it will be more messed up than before. Lord, I tried to keep my head held high but with all these bumps and bruises, I left with a migraine.

I tried to do my best in all areas in my life, yet somewhere down the line, I messed up. Lord, please forgive me and how do I forgive myself? Constantly beating myself up for the bad decisions I made. Lord, teach me how to get through this and be more aware of you.

I've been down to my last count before, but this round I can't make it without you. So take my hand precious Lord and lead me through, teach me how to forgive, to love, and to never forget how you brought me through!

SELF-DESTRUCTION

Paving the way to a dark road where we never wanted to be, but the trials and tribulation had me ready to explode. Back and forth, I go pleading and begging to pass this heavy cup from me, I couldn't take it anymore.

This season brought more than tears, had me on my hands and knees: trying to gain understanding of this season and its purpose. Through the night I cried hoping that some light would beam down to clear the way; forgetting about the promises made, all I could see was chaos, confusion, and pain.

As I got before the Lord, this time I had to strip myself of the weight and say,

"Lord, I don't know what you're doing, but I want all of You. I trust you because I'm empty."

I was at a place that was leading me in the path that would promote self-destruction. However, the love of the Father removes me from that path into a more in-depth walk with Him. No longer letting my circumstances consume me, but pressing harder toward the prize, thank you Lord for sparing my life!

LORD, HOLD IT ALL BACK

Lord, hold back my tears. I can't waste another day.
> I tried to pray but the enemy's voice kept
> telling me no way, and that you don't
> hear me anyway.

Lord, hold back my pain. I'm trying to forget
about all the hurt and shame.

It feels as if the clothes I wear are tainted by
my shame.

Just hide me for a little while 'til the pain
subsides within.

Lord, hold back all the hindrances that kept
me from you.

I fell too many times trying to live
right without you.

Change my life with just one touch and fill
that bottomless void.

I can't do anything, but wait on you, Oh my Lord.

Perseverance

I tried to do it my way, but my life was
still incomplete.

I'm in need of your guidance from my head
to my feet.

I want to walk opposite of you, but that
just won't do.

So, I'm backing up and giving it all to you.

Lord, hold me back from the enemy's hands
who plots to take my life.

I believe that when I abide in you that everything
will be alright.

No longer bound by the enemy words, they
are just hearsays.

But the words of the one true power has saved
me for another day!

Kelamenter M. Smith

REACH OUT AND TOUCH

Reach out and touch me Lord.

    My mind was wandering astray.
I've made some terrible decisions with a
heavy price to pay.
I wanted to run and hide, but a preacher
led me to you.
They said you will take all my guilt and shame
away if I confess, repent, and accept you.

I prayed:

"Lord of heaven, I repent of my sins that I did. I want to be renewed. I tried to do things my way, but became more misunderstood. People looked at me as if I'm a criminal, but that's not me. I've made bad mistakes listening to the wrong baritone, when I should've listened to the One from heavens' throne. But now I know that it was you that kept me all my days.

Remembering that one night I thought I was going to die, but you reached out and touched me, my body was healed inside. I want to feel that touch again every-day of the week. I don't want to fall again, staggering trying to keep my feet."

Father in heaven, I accept all of you, come into my life because nothing else will do. Wash me Lord from top to bottom, I want you only, to be my Almighty Tower keeping watch over my soul. Thank you for the blood that made me whole. No longer feeling demise in guilt, but I rise in Him who was Heaven sent!

IN THE MIDNIGHT HOUR

It is in the midnight hour when the saints begin to cry. Lord all I want is you, you are my healing power. Lately to me I can't see my way, Lord hear my cry for this day has gotten the best of me. I want to forget about the disappointments that came my way.

I need a peace of mind for what's ailing me. I realize that, when I stopped running I was able to hear you. I gained more valuable news, I want to bust loose.

Touch me Lord while I pray, make me better by your saving grace. Heal me and make me complete, knowing what the shed blood of Christ truly means. The ultimate sacrifice and the Heavens still sing.

What a wonderful experience to hear, let my light be that example to share of that glorious day. I was picked up out of the darkness and saved from the grave. You washed me and purified me to be presented before the throne. Heaven is my goal, my heavenly home.

Here I stand pondering "Why at midnight and the significance it has to me." This is when the terror comes because darkness cannot conqueror light, but light always outshines the darkness!

"You're here to be light, bringing out the God-colors in the world, God is not a secret to be kept."

Matthew 5:14-16, Peterson, (2002).

Kelamenter M. Smith

YOU SEEM FAR AWAY

Two steps forward as I look for you, but where are you? Reminiscing of the time we shared, I'm sorry I left so soon, But now I want to bet near you. I've searched high and low trying my best to get back to where we used to be. Please somebody help me!

I'm sorry I left the way I did and not believing you know what's best for me. Thinking I could handle it all on my own, I was wrong and I need you badly.

My love, to me you seem so far away from my reach, my touch, and my soul. Please come to me so that I can feel you again. Your gentle breeze that puts my mind at ease, I miss that feeling of being whole.

I apologize for being out of line when you were showing me that it wasn't my time. I fainted and fussed, but now looking to you. I don't want to be in this miserable distress anymore. So Lord if you hear me please let me know you're here. I will not leave until I feel your touch again!

THE WILLOW TREE TEARS TOUCH ME

As I lay against the tall green tree thinking of all the disappointments and pain last year. While slowly drifting off to sleep. I cried out,

"Why did I have to go through all the mess and misery?"

The visions of different events that took place made me realize that God led me through a safer route, but with a lesson to learn. Now I see why they called the issues of life growing pains. Then I was shown the direction as a result of making bad choices.

All I could say was, "Thank you Father."

I didn't realize the many consequences of one bad decision affect others. I sat up quickly knowing that it was more than a dream, but a reality.

From regrets to rejoice, now I can truly say, if it had not been for God's love, mercy, and grace I would not be here today. Wiping away the moisture on my face and looking up to see:

Even the compassionate tears from the
willow tree have touched me!

Kelamenter M. Smith

DAILY I WALK

I desire daily to walk with you leading the way. My mind is sometimes clouded when I cannot decide which road to take, but with you leading me, I am on a path called straight. Take me to a higher place to be secure with your glory. Nothing can't compare to the moments that is shared with you.

Grateful for each waking day, wanting all my mornings to live in the presence of peace and my nights to be embraced by your protective wings of love. Just one more moment, one more step of fulfilling my aspirations that burn within. Reaching the height and depths of your Holy manifestation that alwaysbrings life and grace again.

No longer accepting what seems normal, but looking at the impossible; that you can make possible to a forsaken land. Daily striving for the goal that was set before me, I'm not worried about the headaches that the world always brings. As I look to you for a new beginning, trusting in your true power, and the Almighty word that is for us.

Daily I walk, thinking of you and the gracious gifts you always give. With each passing day I leap with joy, of the countless blessings, I will praise your name. You have done so much for me, even when I was at my lowest You still came to see about me.

Kelamenter M. Smith

Living the rest of my life trying to repay you,

Pleasing you, wanting to do more and more just for you.

Teary eyes of pain and disappointments have gone away.

For I have a future and a hope in the one who has made this life worth enduring.

So goodbye old sorrows, goodbye old pains, hello sunshine and refreshing rain.

And always enjoying being in your presence, Lord, You are my everything!

THE VALUE OF ME

When you look in the mirror what do you see?

Do you see the beautiful King or Queen the Heavenly Father wanted you to be?

How do you see yourself?

Is it from the outside-in or inside-out?

Do you take on how others see you?

Or are you searching for the real you?

Does expensive clothes make you valuable or is it the opposite?

Just like updates to a home, do you hold yourself devalued because of the lack of updates toward self-improvement?

So what is your value?

I am more valuable than expensive clothes.

I am more than the car I drive.

I am more than the shoes I wear.

I am more than the residence I live in.

I am more than the business I own.

Kelamenter M. Smith

I am more than the name I hold.

I am more than a pretty face, tight waist, or not.

I am more than a job title/name.

I am more than the skills I obtain.

I am more than my circumstance.

~

But, let me tell you how valuable I am.

I am a child of a Supreme Father who loves me.

I am a joint-heir with Christ, my King.

I am a part of a royal family.

I am spiritually and wonderfully made.

I am a chosen generation.

I am blessed and highly favored.

I am more than a conqueror.

I am valuable to the most High, and to me.

Therefore, don't let others try to reduce you to nothing with their mind games. You are better than that, you belong to the Almighty King. You are a priceless gem brought with His life, so don't allow yourself and others to belittle your value. I belong to the Omnipotent Being that loves me so much and teaches me the value of ME!

FROM THE CRIB THEY CRY

From generation to generation the pain still stands, from east to west, from north to south. All cries are the same and nothing really changed. In a city, slowly disintegrating and the politicians don't really care. No one to blame, no help, no hope, or no love to gain.

From the crib they cry, when the young die before the old. From the crib they cry, when the heart isn't strong enough to hold a rhythm or a note. From the crib they cry, when out of the womb to an early tomb. No one can explain the hurt and misery from light to gloom.

From the crib they cry, when their bodies are wracked in pain, begging for hope and a bit of relief. From the crib they cry, slowly dying and they don't know why, but their reality is:

"When will it be my time to die?"

In a city gradually wasting away, the city that was once the place to be has turned its back against the innocent. The cries are louder than their song, but no one is concern about their agony.

From the crib they cry, when their eyes are swollen from tears pleading for mercy but not sure who to plead to. Their only thought is: "Can you please help me?" From the crib they cry, when abuse has no standards and no age limit is required.

From the crib they cry, when they are taught how to get high before they reach five. From the crib they cry, when they cried out "why God why?" When they knew it wasn't God they wanted when they are not in trouble.

Too many of us think that we can do whatever we want without consequences, truth be told. There are many who think that they're above God, when it is from the dust we rose, and back to the dust we lay. From the crib they cry and fight to live another day; pray to the Heavenly Father to keep you always!

THE SILENT KILLER

He lurks about the universe in search for his next prey. His sneaky smile would be a dead giveaway, if his victims could only see him. Each time he subdues his martyr, he prances around like he just conquered the world.

Yet he still thinks that he won, and the rest will be defeated. If he could have his way, it would be like the silent killer that flows through darkness quietly snatching lives left and right.

His movement would be like a fog that blankets the land. However, we should be glad that, through all that he does, He still must obtain permission for touching those things, which is not his. His temper tantrum is concealed for the physical eyes to see, using cancer as his device. It is like kryptonite to Superman; this evil device brings us to our knees.

The device is chipping away our defenses, our hopes, our dreams, our loved ones, our bodies, our six senses, our minds, our love for the Most High, and our souls. Even though the pain that caped our bodies, we lie there perplexed about the situation. Our thinking cap has given us a long-term commitment in the same area, so it would seem.

Kelamenter M. Smith

Longevity in other remote areas has dispelled itself from us, yet the fight continues for life. As cumbersome as the situation is, we are not the one for giving up easily.

It may seem hopeless to remain this way, but hope in conjunction with faith is what is keeping us in this trial. We learned that the Father would never put more on you than you can bear. So, stay in the race for the work is not through, there is need of you. If only you will trust the process, He will bring you through!

FILL THIS EMPTY VESSEL

Down in what seems like the bottom of the barrel, there is no way I am letting this get to me. Down in what should be like my last meal, is an appetizer for the main course. Down in what felt like the end of my knotted rope, was an added extension for me to hold on longer.

When you pour out so much of yourself into what was less important, you tend to fill empty. Yet still searching for something or someone to fill you. When the Master is waiting for you to come to Him and run into his open arms.

When you pour out so much of yourself into a job that will not elevate you nor congratulate you, it seems less important to you anymore. Nonetheless, the void in you is expanding to the point you just␣what to be made whole again.

Searching in all the wrong places, smiling in everyone faces, but there is one you have not turned to. He is waiting for you and what you to himself, he is the best and there is none like him. When going to the altar, I place myself upon your feet saying, fill me with you.

LIVING BEYOND SELF: Searching For Meaning

Lord, every corner of my life has been cluttered without you and now I know I am lost without you. Fill up the emptiness with your love and amazing grace, I recognize I need you.

Life is not worth living without you. Your anointing spirit has rivers of living water, so please fill this empty vessel. Nothing can change my mind about you, now that I am free. Free to love, free to worship you, free to live the way Christ showed me, and free to be a new me. Therefore, fill up this vessel and pour out your overflow, then others will know this is not a no-show.

Let your light so shine through me that others will see, I walk this walk not alone, but by the Spirit of God that lives within me!

THE PRICE WAS PAID: NOT BY YOU

The sudden impact of a difficult moment steals the achievement of joy in an instant. The realization of all the hopes and dreams faded into darkness because of the ill-gotten mistake of trusting the wrong being.

The warning was there, you just couldn't see it, blinded by the fabrication of what looks appealing to the eyes was bad for the soul.

The massive abrasive in your spirit cause you to weep for the comfort of the Savior, nonetheless you knew deep down inside it was wrong. The price for satisfying the flesh is worse than lusting after the flesh.

What is so darn great about being satisfied in sin? Nothing. What is so hard about following the Master Creator that we say, "seeing is believing?" Trust is the key factor, along with faith.

The repeated cycle that derail our lives cause by self-inflicted, generational curses, and other unholy venom has indeed slowly drained our confidence in the Truth of Great I AM. The lack of knowledge, will power, faith the size of a mustard seed, and forgiveness has taken its toll in majority of life situations.

Yet the repeat words "Is Your all on the Altar of sacrifice laid." Put aside your troubles to the one that has conquered and defeated the enemy's plan. It was by the blood that redemption was made and the price was paid. Therefore, every situation was nailed to the cross that day, not by you but for you. Therefore, why do we insist on doing it our way, which causes more harm than good? Look deep into the price that was paid for your salvation and learn to appreciate the only one that gave it all for so little.

He left his home in glory, to bring man back to him and made life a valuable gem. He has proven what no others can, his saving grace, and his redeeming power that saved man!

I SEE NOTHING'S CHANGED

I thought for sure that there was a hint of change, but the reality is that vision that I thought I saw was a lie. Boldly the facade comes off like a scalp, slowly dropping for the real deal to show, and I see that nothing's changed.

I thought for sure that this was a different phase in time, a different season, and a different life, I was wrong. The same issues, the same disappointments, and pain, masquerade until due time to peek its ugly head out for the true face to show. Now I know and I see that nothing's changed.

The sneaky traps that the enemy uses to distract, discourage, and disassemble the growing mantle of faith, which you tried to build has tumbled. In what seems like a simple dispute, turned into an all-out war, which had nothing to do with the starting line anyway.

Too many lives have been shattered by the very chaos that seeks to confuse and eliminate the very wholesome nature you try to build and rebuild. It is like that crow that keeps coming back pecking away at the same target to tear down its defenses. The enemy uses your weakness to bring you to a halt. As if knowing this and you do not seek strength in that area, how then can you pray for help?

LIVING BEYOND SELF: Searching For Meaning

I thought for sure that these childish ways were a thing of the past, now I see that nothing's changed. It hurts to see that everything is the same and no one wants to accept their own blame, but ready to point out and accuse the other for their pain, isn't that a shame?

> When do we look in the mirror and see our own guilt, frustration, and pain?
>
> Do I blame the one in the mirror for the years' worth of hurt and pain?
>
> Do I cry out to those I dare not name?
>
> Do I just confess and admit the truth that, it wasn't you?
>
> Where is the Love?
>
> Where can I hide to gain a peaceful mind until this thunderstorm rolls away?

Lord, I pray that you will help us find that peaceful place in you. Lord, cleanse us from the things of the past and refresh us then to make us anew. Let your will be done as we bring all things back unto you.

Kelamenter M. Smith

Empty our minds of worldly idle and fill it with you, for we are far better when we follow you. No longer do I want to see the same old tired things, replenish my eyes to see things in you made new. No compromise, no hustling, we will have to do, but *"every good and perfect gift comes from above."* James 1:17 (NIV).

As we lay our weary head, let us rest in you, no one can give us sweet sleep like you. Thank you Lord for listening to a heartfelt prayer, I will do my best to be what you call me to be. Covered in your fruits of the Spirit let it all take place. Change me for the greater race you position me for a greater place!

STEP ASIDE

Buried in past mistakes, my eyes they did cry in wanting the pain to roll away. Looking to others for help, but no one can truly console me. Ashamed by the disgrace that came when my innocence was betrayed, my eyes they did cry.

Oh, wretched man is he who has spoiled my purity and cause me harm. Why, O why must you come flexing your strong arm, isn't it enough that I bear the pain from an adolescent to the teenage years. Why must you force your evil acts upon me?

As the nighttime falls and my tear stained eyes close into a somnolent state, wishing this pleasant vision don't go away. The sunlight rays hit my face and awaken back into reality. Bursting into tears saying, "Why it is me that has to experience this doom? Am I marked with a curse because there is no love here for me to bloom?"

Falling deep into prayer as the rivers from my eyes is shed; please take me from this misery and despair. Lord, if you are real and hear my plea; please don't let this go on no more, Lord please.

Perseverance

Drifting off to sleep was as sweet as the morning dew,
but the voice that came to me made me afraid to move.

"My Child, God has seen your tears and felt your
pain, step aside and know your Heavenly Father
cares. He will make the bittersweet taste go away
and fill it with sweet honeycomb, and the warmth
of His embrace.

So, close your eyes the day draws near,
rest my dear and sleep in peace, for a better
tomorrow is at its peak.

Just rest in the Lord and
leave all your burdens there.

Vengeance is His thus says The Lord.
Step Aside and you will see the
Lord's mighty hand at work in thee!"

Kelamenter M. Smith

DISCOLORATIONS

The dissatisfaction of walking into destiny, but it does not feel like it is mine. Am I walking into a black and white movie, yet in present time? Do mine eyes deceive me from the youthfulness of light and life? What is the thing that causes dissimulation, when the facts are lay before me?

Yet more wasted time that has gone by while wondering if these frustrations were the reason to leave. The disconnection and the disbelief have taken its toll on me, but I will try to stay and fight to win.

I sit, I cry, I sit, and I cry again, what I can do to make this nightmare end? Sleeping in hopeless nights and no cover to pull over me to hide my bulging eyes. Yet you try to save face with a slanted smile.

Not much for company, nor for conversation between the two, you rather it be me and you. Here lies a wasted gift with no pizzazz for life, it moseys on by like a snail in a race. The very thought of you seems to fade my mind when I think of your Dr. Jekyll and Mr. Hyde disguise.

You had me fooled and dumbfounded too, I thought for sure I knew you. Using your enchanted words and no-fault tales, had me disillusionary in my mind.

>How can I get to the betterment of me when the thick layers of lies and deceit overthrow me?

Distant memories of what used to be, has me in a faded gray area wishing for sunlight to touch me. This taint the world has stamped me with their discoloration of love, but mine eyes were closed unto the blood.

Pure and holy, sacred and true, how I hope that one day the blood will purify me again. Now days are short and no era is the same, this one is worse yet no one wants the blame.

No peace, no hope, and no love to share, are we exempt of our rightful share? Infatuation is out the door, it's the heaviness of lust that the world endures. Rain down and cleanse the earth, remember to remove the filth away. Restore mine eyes to see the beauty in life once again!

MY FLESH WENT SUICIDAL

They knew you were no good for me, but the connection between us would not break. Running around rapidly and foolishly searching for love in all the wrong places, and in the wrong faces.

Flirting with destruction was just foreplay, but the main event was pure evil. Chaos was the entree and conceptualizing every emotion that is negative and turn it into a collage of malice in all affairs.

They knew you were no good for me the moment you spotted me. I was your main target, or at least that is how it felt to me. Everything came caving in upon my shoulders, my mind took a long ride on the roller coaster.

Back and forth as I pace the floor, pleading for a way to escape this madness. I stop, laugh, and then I cried, I laughed again at the very thought of myself.

As loud as I could, I yelled "I quit." My love for the Heavenly Father is worth more than losing myself in this world. My flesh was itching to do its own thing, but I refuse to live the same. I asked the Father to do an inward change, now my life won't be the same again!

ALL GLAMOUR BUT NO BRAINS

Are you what they say about you, or are you the opposite of what they say?

Who are you or do you know?

You live in a fantasy world that everyone ought to cater to you. However, what do you give to others and do you cater to them as well? Well we must admit you look the part, but the reality is you are no different from the politicians, who say they cannot tell a lie; the fact remains that it is a lie.

You can pretend all you want, but the lie is still the same. You play mind games as if it is your own personal toy, but once exposed you're ready to explode. Silly rabbit tricks are for kids and you got me confused with those idiots you are use to.

Your glamorous looks will not get you far and to others it is a no-brainer. You thought it was all about you, but in the end, it is all glamour and no brains. Therefore, stop trying to live like the rich and famous with God because you will pay for idol worshipping. By making everything else your god but the Almighty God!

THE WANDERER

The dust from this walk has blown in my eyes; now the irritation and the minor burning sensation causes me to cry. This feeling of lack has me all twisted up inside not knowing if today will be my last supper and then I die.

No, I still have work left in me to do, besides it costs too much to die, so I might as well keep pushing on and live. The limited resources have not increased and I'm wondering why. All I'm trying to do is get above water, but it still feels like I'm being pulled down.

No food, no rest, no peace, no sleep, and not a place to lay our head; the taste of desolation has gripped me once more. This area I know all too well, yet I'm left feeling, looking, and living like the wanderer saying "Lord, are you there?"

Sometimes it feels like I'm in a dry land and when looking at the situation, I'm in a place called "I'm barren." So where has my seed gone? I try to toil day and night, but the results are still the same. What can I do to bring about a change? All I want was a little bit of heaven here on Earth. Yet waiting for that dream to come true, seeing everyone get a blessing except you.

I wonder what will become of the Wanderer, this I do not know. I pray that the God of Heaven will release some joy upon me and open a window or a door. Lord, fill me again and make me complete with you. Take hold of my situation because I have nothing left within. Free me from myself so that I can fly again.

No longer, am I the Wanderer as I once used to be but regaining the vision of the person God wants me to be. No longer afraid of what the world thinks of me, I am no longer their priority. Walking with a new agenda and a smile on my face, basking in God's glory and in His amazing grace!

THE BARREN TREE

I am not the barren tree that stands there lifeless and dry wishing for time to bloom, but nothing has survived.

    I am not the barren tree that lies in wait
    Something or someone to bring it to life.

    I am not the barren tree that hopes to one day prosper,
    yet never produces any fruit.

    But I am the tree that has been picked at,
    talked about, and misused.

Yet, I am not withering away from my purpose. I am pruned so that the best in me will flourish for the Father. It doesn't matter what man may say, it only matters what God says. My tree does not shake to the whistling winds, but stands firm even in adverse seasons.

I am a tree; steady, blooming with a purpose to fulfill, not made by man. But for the One who created me and filled me with a divine destiny.

Moreover, every tree has been plant with purpose, it's in due season that the tree blossoms in which it was designed for by the Master. It was said, *"You'll recognize them by their fruit."* Matt.7:16 (HCS).

So I'm to live a life that is pleasing to God and not to the world. My journey is to bring glory to God and not to man. Designed and formed by the Creator of all the one that gives love, life, and liberty!

Kelamenter M. Smith

THE END — RESULTS

Whenever someone testifies about a blessing they received, it is the result of holding on through the trial and tests. Whenever someone you know gain more favor than you do, it is the result of being obedient and faithful during the storm.

We are privileged to see the results of our future, but no one wants the trial period that we must go through to get the blessing. The story of Joseph and all that he went through was hidden to him. The only thing God shown Joseph was the end—results thereof.

We can all relate to a dream or a vision where an end—result is given to us or we see the future results, but not the process we must go through. Whatever is shown to you, seek God in all things and strength for the journey, and know that God desire to bless you not to curse you!

THE UNTHINKABLE

It's sad to say but yeah you got played all while you thought I was down. Now, whose face is left on the ground, feeling like a dud, like the fool you are. What you thought might have worked out for you turned out to be a lie.

You see I may not hold all the cards, but I know the one that does. So, I did what anyone would do, it's not elementary my dear. You better get up out of here because as far as I'm concern you are through.

You pretend to run with the best, yet still in all it was not enough for you to cut a deal. My stakes ride high and you could not comply. I went to the One that caught more than my eye but stole my heart. Therefore, I did the unthinkable and united we are. The love of my life and even death cannot depart.

So goodbye, so long it was a treat, but this love has loved me throughout eternity. Bound by this feeling, I do not want it to end. I vow never ever to leave you again. Take me up and soothe my soul, refresh me within and make me whole.

You complete me like no other can, yet I am at a loss for words at the touch of your hands. Because every time I cry, you wipe away my tears and tell myself,

"It is going to be okay and do not fret my dear."

How can I not love you and those special
moments we share?

I looked at myself and wondered why me, why was I the one you wanted to be with. At that time, I did not feel special enough to be your queen. However, you showed true love and my life has not been the same. There is not a single moment that I would not trade for the world.

You make this life worth fighting for and with you, I am Victorious!

THIS FIGHT JUST GOT REAL

You question the facts that spread through this life, about life. Not everything you thought was legit, is. You ask for directions from those who are far, far, behind, yet you're wondering:

"How can I get mine?"

Distant memories from the past seem to bombard your mind into overloading, you are trying to grasp on to something profound and true. Even the past had tainted glass, yet you managed to see it through. Scattered pictures and broken dreams is all you seem to see.

Whatever happen to that saying, "Leap before you cross?"

Bet you nine times out of ten you were strutting your stuff like a superstar. Yet still in the struggle and you begin to ponder each day more and more. If your destiny was just a mirage or something, you had hoped for.

Every-day you go back and forth, over and over in your mind; "Lord, are you real or am I just wasting my time? Am I glutton for punishment because that's all I seem to know?"

You tried to relax, but it became more intense, when the war came to your door. Now you're really wondering:

"How can this be or am I just another pawn
in this crazy game?"

When looking at both sides, you're contemplating which one will win. It never occurred to you despite it all that this fight just got real.

No rulebooks, no playbooks, or no coach qualified to console you. You look toward the sky and say, "My God, Why?" But, who are you talking to if He doesn't know you. The pain, the agony, the guilt, and the shame of never taking the time to truly glorify His name.

Now you are pleading before the Judge comes, desiring to soothe the pain. Realizing that your case will go to trial, while the guilty charge is on the table for the whole world to see. The enemy had the upper hand on you, yet Jesus can break you free.

So, call upon Him and repent of your sins, allow the refreshing of your soul to take place. Renew your mind, read the fine lines, and know that God is still in control. Take nothing for granted because each day is not promised to you. Take a good hard look from what God has brought you through. Be thankful for the time you have now and the given task, at hand. If you are not careful, it could be you on the breaking end!

DO YOU CARE?

The road of destruction is an open and easy way to go. Many have already traveled this way, whether willingly or unwillingly, but only the Father knows. So, do you care enough to share with others the way to a more seclude, secured, and elite road to go? Not everyone is going. But if you let me show you "better," will you go?

The examples for us paved the way, but the thought of never being satisfied creeps in like a black cat. It looks for the "better" when, what we have been told, is better. Therefore, you do care a little, to point others to the One that has a history of problem solving and recovery. If you will, there is room for more. There is no discrimination; this is an equal opportunity for all race, creed, and ages.

The map has been established and validated for the journey, which is laid long before us. Yet we are still confused about the journey or suffer from the lack of knowledge of the Truth. The cost has been paid for you, so you are more than welcome to come along. Just understand that you're not in it alone, there is help available for you.

Do you care enough to assist others, or is it a self-sufficient exhibition? What would you do to help your family, your friends, or even your enemies reach the final destination, or do you care? Christ does, so how about you!

SWEET DREAMS

Sweet dreams my love as you drift off to sleep. May your head rest easy and your mind gain peace. Sweet dreams my darling as your body's strength is restored. May the angels from heaven watch over you.

With each passing day while working toward your goal, you wonder has anything changed for you. It seems like this work has caused nothing but confusion, frustration, and disappointment. Yet, determined to continue to work and walk through this pain.

Days at a time, you pray for a little relief and each morning you are stronger and stronger. So be encouraged while you go through this season, trust in God for there is always a reason.

Sweet dreams my love as you rock yourself to sleep know that God's angels have been set to keep you. Sweet dreams my sweet and put your day to rest. You have only the one who can do more than open a window, or a door of blessings. He can create an opportunity that is not of this but through Him, anything is possible. Therefore, keep yourself in the Lord's will and continue to dress yourself with the armor of the Father as you walk the path that is laid out before you.

Perseverance

Sweet dreams my darling as the angels encamp around you. Know that the peace of God flows through your home and rest assured that the Father is working for your good!

LIVING BEYOND SELF: Searching For Meaning

WHEN THE TEARS SEEMS TO FLOW

The years seem to get rougher and rougher, yet still trying to smile. You try to get a handle on the situation but more issues stack up. The tears flow heavy as you look up wondering "Why?" but there is no clue, no answer, and no sound.

The pain becomes unbearable when it starts to feel like a rending of your flesh. The storms that come have been designed just for you, so you think "Am I the only one going through this type of issue?"

We all have seasons that we must prevail but there is a sure thing that God is able. So hold on to this insurance for your assurance. Just when you are at the brink and want to give in, God steps in, and saves you.

The love of the Father is just that powerful to help you in all seasons, and still see about others. Therefore, when the tears begin to flow, in your mind your questioning what to do, reach out to the Father, and he will talk to you!

WAKE ME WHEN THIS IS OVER

I sat in a still room as the house lay to rest, imaging the future life I would like to live in. Then the voice said, "Get your head out of the clouds that will never be." Looking at your 'here and now', you will never get there."

What a cruel and twisted deception, but not a surprise. I rebuked that voice and spoke words of positive empowerment. The reflection of Christ attributes became clear to me.

As we continue to grow in Christ, we are no longer searching within ourselves for answers. When the answers are accessible, all we have to do was "ask" but our approach can be a little offensive toward the Heavenly Father. Therefore, I ask the Father to teach me how to approach Him correctly, and that is pleasing to Him.

For a while, I was used to just knocking on the door, but no one would answer, every once in a while. It was so frustrating that I was at a point to say, "Just wake me when this is over." But it is not this day, I've changed the channel and dial tone: familiarizing myself with the Masters' love and voice!

Kelamenter M. Smith

FLASHBACKS ARE HEAVY HITTERS

The light shines between my eyes; I am blinded by the view of my future. However, my very present state holds me in a momentary stand still. I can't move, can't hardly breathe, nor can I feel anything.

This grip is tighter than a twist cap on a bottle of soda pop. There was no space to move just locked-in and my eyes were too. The stiffness causes me not to grit my teeth nor clinch my fist. Do I want to move? "Yes!" Do I want to be free? "Yes!" I stand in a frozen state, wondering what is wrong with me.

I wanted to scream, but who would hear me? My voice is dry as sandpaper, no words would come out. I closed my eyes and stayed there, and then it finally hit me. So hard that it would have knocked me down, not that I was impressed, but it was something simple.

The calm still voice comes with power and authority that sent chills all over my body. The voice says, "I am the beginning and the end, I have rights, authority, and power over all. So why are you consumed in your present that you forget about your future I have shown you? This, my child is not your end; you still have work to do and know that I am always within reach. You just have to believe and trust in Me!"

FINAL FAREWELL TO YOUR PAST

Now is the time to release yourself from your past. Good riddance, goodbye to the many scars that are held in your heart, those memories that reminds you of the pain. Oh, how you desire to put your mind at ease, no longer held captive by its darkened ways that would keep you caged.

Now set free and clear to say "You are no longer bound to your past, but you're escalating toward your future. Your past held you in that place of hurt, disappointment, bitterness, and confusion for far too long. However being in that environment is a thing of the past. You are free!"

Wholeheartedly you can exclaim, "So long, farewell to your painful past. Your lasting grip is not equipped to hold me down. My future holds greater rank than you. Therefore, I leave you right where you belong and I will only hold on to the good times."

You have no dominion nor free reign, I will not be taken captive again by you. My strength is renewed and my mind is alert, my eyes are open and I have changed my view. I see a brighter future rather than the dark and hurtful past. I'm finally free at last!

IN SEARCH OF ME

As a child, you're taught how to behave.

    What you should wear or what you shouldn't wear.

    What you can or cannot say.

    What you can or cannot do.

    So the question is "Who are you?"

You can stand in front of the mirror daily. It still won't change the fact that you're a different vessel of your parents' character. But you've taken so much of their traits, their habits, and their style You almost forgot who you are.

    No frills, no fillers, nor imitations needed.

    No clones, no drones, or wannabees.

No duplication, no recreation, or stunt doubles of me.

    I'm the only one with my DNA, I AM ME.

No liars, no sidewinders, or cheap moments of thrills.

    No stomach aching, no body shaking, or pill
        taking to say the least.

No night walking, no jive talking, or cutting it too close.

To be honest with you anyway, I never was about that hood life. I'm just trying to live my life the best way I can. Nor am I interested in trying to oust "The Man." This man has nothing on me, nor can he come against me.

I'm a creation full of purpose and awaits destiny
in search of me!

UNDER PRESSURE

Day by day you live in a self-contained shell. Where you feel like the more the pressure builds, the harder it gets. You're wondering how long before it blows. The balancing act of keeping your cool would be an understatement. You were told to always prepare for the worst. Yet you wonder "Why" the worst will come whether you want it or not You would rather strive for better.

Day by day you live in a self-contained shell. Where you feel like the more the pressure builds the harder it gets. You feel as though the walls will close in on you at any given moment. When all you wanted to do was live right, do right, and get in right standing. But now you question every move whether it's by you or others. You even question the true motives beyond their actions.

Day by day, month by month, and year to year, you pray that the release of peace will continue to flow through you. Understand that you're not alone, but there's comfort at the end of this journey!

SUDDEN IMPACT

It happens so quickly, like a blink of an eye we didn't see this coming at all. But here is the story:

The feeling of urgency in your spirit awakens you at exactly 3:44 a.m. for two weeks straight. You knew something was going on because you didn't miss a beat. It was exactly 3:44 a.m. You sat up straight from a somber sleep, but you got up and prayed. However, by the second week there is a lump in your throat before uttering a prayer. You're wondering, "Lord what's going on?"

So instead of praying, you sit there meditating on the goodness of Jesus. Nonetheless, for that whole week you sit up meditating on the Word of God, not saying anything just sitting there.

Now don't get me wrong my flesh wanted to go back to sleep, but when you are awakened at a specific time for two weeks straight you ought to take heed. Remember when doing the work of the Lord God, it's not about you. After the two-week period of 3:44 a.m. wake-up experiences, ponder which leads to you praying in the Spirit.

The realization is God was preparing you for what seemed like a sudden impact. We couldn't believe what we heard; just recently we spoke over the phone. Not long after the sting that came quickly pierce our hearts. The grief of not being there sooner gripped me so hard that I wanted to scream. But I knew she understood, sadden that I couldn't give her one last kiss goodbye I cried.

Nonetheless, remembering she was a praying woman of God. So as the family lives out the remainder of their days, let's strive harder to increase in the kingdom of God. We have work to do in the name of the Lord Jesus! Amen!

RESCUE MISSION

The swirl of dust spins around as the helicopter lands. The voices sound familiar, but you can't make them out. The muffled ringing in your ears, your eyes can barely stay open as your body screams in agony. You're wondering what happened, what went wrong as you lay limp from the disheartening situation.

You see lights flashings, radios playing, and people in blue, black, and white uniforms moving fast around you. You hear the words. "Can you hear me?" "Can you see me?" Yet your throat barely releases the words, but you manage to say "Yes." Then all of a sudden, you're being moved onto a bed. The doctors are yelling medical utterance you can't understand.

The nurses check your vitals as you're being rushed into the room. However, that one whisper declares "You're going to be OK." The feeling of sweat, tears, blood, and pain has filled not only your body but your lips as well. You wanted to wail because of the misery you're in, but the soothing injected medication helps you relax. But now in dreamland, you're running around chasing and playing with the children. All happy thoughts play in your mind over and over again. Then suddenly it hits you and the memories rush back in your mind like a mighty raging river; all you could think about was "Lord please help me."

The picture became clearer and as the memories are recalibrating quickly your body jerked. You hear the doctors saying, "Her body is going into shock" as the moments become prolonged. After an hour of calming your body down the medical team was able to seal all wounds and place you in the recovery room.

You awake in three days later, with a loud shout "Jesus!" As the nurses bombards the room, your arms stretch out as you look up saying "Thank you." You ask the nurse what happen, and she said "Sweetie you were in a bad accident trying to save a little child." So, you ask, "Did she survive?" and the nurse smiled and said "Yes, yes you did" and walked out.

The moral of this story is we spend majority of our lives trying to find that missing piece but nothing seems to fit. We tend to cling to people, things, and ideas but disregard the One True Source to us all. We were willing to try any and everything to make life work, but fail to recognize your true You.

How many times has God saved you from yourself? Romans 10:13 *"For everyone who calls on the name of the Lord will be saved."* (HCSB).

The thing is we don't know we need rescuing until it is too late. We become blindsided by the world's illusions. We don't recognize our true nature and for which it stands. How can we lead others to Christ to be saved when we ourselves need saving?

Jesus rescues us from an everlasting torment and redeems us to God. Now we can choose to live accordingly and partake of eternal life. Earth is temporal, Heaven is always!

THE UPSIDE DOWN OF THINGS

For the past eight years in my life has been more challenging than I had ever imagined. I mean new experiences of rejection, pain, death, love, happiness, sadness, and the unfamiliar. The changes in relationships both physical and spiritual, I never thought I would end up here...so here I am.

The reality is so perplexing until it makes me wonder if in fact I am living in a distorted dream trying to escape. It's funny how things you never hoped for come, and the things you hoped for are a distant goal. You're wondering if you're standing, or staying in the right place, afraid to move even an inch in fear that you might miss out on the one thing that can change your entire situation.

I have often heard and read, "If God be for us who can be against us." Well it's a great thing that God is always for me to excel and not fail, or else I would be steering in that direction. No, I'm not saying I'm a failure; just some of the decisions made throughout this life have failed me. But, like they say, "knowing is half the battle" the other half of the battle is making it through to the finish line.

Picture this: Everything was going great and everything in your area is falling in line. The job, education, family, friends, and even your enemies behaved. Then one day, it is like you stepped into a different time zone or something. Everything is affected, the home, the family, the job, friends, enemies, and yourself.

You look and wonder what in the world is going on, it's like you walked into a long nightmare that will not let up. Until one day you just spent a whole day praying over every situation, every curse, every disease, every family, every illness, every job, every surgeon, every hospital, and everything worth praying over.

By then you're exhausted and ready to lie down when another prayer request is asked of you, what do you do? Everything around you is spinning and barely able to move, when you say a brief prayer something sparks within your spirit. The Holy Spirit says, "From the heart does it speak volumes, so whatever you do for God will last." I follow my heart and not my head this time. It felt good to be obedient.

In this adjustment period, I realize that there will be things that appear to look right to the eyes, but be bad for the soul. In Christ there is no middle way, no shortcuts, no hookups, no back ways, no side jobs, and no amount that can be paid. It's a straight shot its either the highway or no way. The Bible tells us that the way is narrow and only a few will make it in. Well I don't know about you, but I definitely want to be one of the few that make it beyond the gates.

So redirecting, reorganizing, rededicating, restyling, refurbishing, and/or renewing my way of thinking and how everything I do and say affects my life, and the lives of others. I don't want anyone connected to me to be hindered because I am not living up to the standard that is set before me. I want to be all that I can be in Christ and to be a Spirit-centered Leader (as Elder Showers would say).

I believe I am more than a conqueror and will have the works to prove otherwise. Therefore, please bear with me because this process takes time, but working to improve for the better and for God to not only use me, but also call upon me after His own Heart!

BIBLIOGRAPHY

Balanced Life Skills. Perseverance Breeds Success Image. Retrieved from balancedlifeskills.com. 2015. Page 81.

Clipart. Heart Image on Page 12. Retrieved from https://www.clipart.email/download/9788426.html.

Etterem.us. Images throughout the book.

Free Vector. Feathered Pen Image on page 69. Retrieved from https://all-free-download.com/free-vector/download/feather-pen_311122.html. 2015.

Freepik.com and etterem.us, Images throughout the book.

Megapixl. Praying Hand Image on Page 4. 2021. Retrieved from https://www.megapixl.com.

Peterson, Eugene H. *The Message Bible*. NavPress, 2002.

Pixabay. Image on Cover and through the book on cover pages. Retrieved from https://pixabay.com/illustrations/dividers-calligraphy-flourish-4869456/.

Shephard, LaShawn. *Helping Others*. Collaboration on page 110, 2008.

The Holy Bible, New King James Version. Nashville: Thomas Nelson Publishers, 1982.

The Holy Bible, Red-letter Edition: Holman Christian Standard Bible. Nashville: Holman Bible Publishers, 2004.

The New International Version Bible. Grand Rapids: Zondervan, 2011.

INSPIRATIONAL NOTE

It is when you start taking God by the hands and see, won't your faith amplified in Him beyond your expectations? Remember you cannot do it alone and you never walk alone as long as you are in Christ Jesus.

My prayer is that we as a whole obtain the mind of Christ and do the work as Christ did. Leaving no souls behind and praying for those that have turned away from Him. Your soul salvation is important to the Body of True Believers in Christ. Just know that you are living with a purpose that only God can show you. May the Most High God keep you and guide you into His Perfect Will.

Kelamenter M. Smith

ABOUT THE AUTHOR

Kelamenter "Kelley" Smith serves in ministry under the leadership of Pastor Corey Sanders of 12:2 Transformation Church. She is an award-winning author who delights herself in sharing inspirational thoughts and Scriptures that apply to life situations. She has a desire to bring forth the creative gifts inside others and shares her love of Christ through words, actions, and deeds.

Having accepted God's call on her life Kelley has been writing since she could remember. Kelley was born and raised inDetroit, MI where she obtained both her Bachelor's degree fromCornerstone University and a Master's degree from South University in Business.

Kelley has been married to Eric for the past 25 years. In this union, they have three adult children, four granddaughters, and a host of adopted children. Prior to this book, Kelley has also published "**Inspirations From The Heart**" & "**Sacred Thoughts: Understanding The Journey.**" She also contributed two poems in the anthology titled: "**The Homeless Cry.**" She has shared her readings on special events.

Smith is a member of the Mentor Empowerment Institute, HOPP Outreach Ministry, Spoken Word Billboard Awards, Poetry Society Association (PSA), and Institute of Real Estate Management (IREM) Associate Member. Smith is planning to release her organization called "The Write 2Nspire."

Kelley has a saying that, "Writing isn't a job or a hobby, it's a lifestyle." As the Lord keeps speaking into her, she will continue to give us encouraging words for the spiritual journey. She knows that through Christ all things are possible.

CONTACT INFORMATION

I look forward to hearing from you. You can contact me about my books, writings, workshops, and conferences. I am available to speak, teach, and for ministry.

Please feel free to contact me at:

http://facebook.com/thewrite2nspire

email me at

write2nspire@gmail.com

OTHER BOOKS WRITTEN BY THE AUTHOR

SACRED THOUGHTS: UNDERSTANDING THE JOURNEY

ISBN: 978-1-60047-421-7

INSPIRATIONS FROM THE HEART

ISBN 1600340784

OTHER BOOKS WRITTEN BY THE AUTHOR

"MY PRAYER TO YOU" & "AMAZING YOU"

Located inside the Anthology **THE HOMELESS CRY**

God Loves You!

NOTES

NOTES

NOTES

www.ingramcontent.com/pod-product-compliance
Lightning Source LLC
Chambersburg PA
CBHW051422290426
44109CB00016B/1404